FAIR CHARTER.

My own model suggestion to update of new Commonwealth nations 2011 (2013 signature of Queen and Prime Ministers) "Charter Of The Commonwealth" constitution in force today for over 2 billion people; You can search this "Charter Of The Commonwealth" document online and see with the Queens official signature and signatures of each of the Prime Ministers of the Commonwealth, arising from my suggestions to Prime Minister Julia Gillard and the Queen for CHOGM 2011 in Perth Australia similar to the Lisbon Treaty of the European Union.

Judgement day; 2017 September 23rd.

By: Lorris Harmlawf. (original author and content, pen name of Loris Erik Kent Hemlof; lekhemlof@gmail.com + lekh@bigpond.com both also for PayPal donations, 42 x 42 phoneme transitions audio http://www.loris-hemlof.com/LEKH-42x42.mp3)

To: Her Majesty The Queen Elizabeth II and Prime Ministers.
And for the benefit of my natural (genetic) family.

FAIR CHARTER (title); Beginning; This FAIR CHARTER for the fair English language Commonwealth Empire; the English Monarch's [Queen Elizabeth II] basic Constitution to which all subsequent legislation in the nation shall move towards compliance to after adoption by the Prime Minister of the English Language Commonwealth Empire nation. Each nations subsequent legislation of each parliament and assembly such as the of the national parliament shall be an easy to read document of (national) laws of up to 100 A4 pages of normal text by the Commonwealth nations national parliament. English Language Commonwealth Empire Citizens Jury update Judgement Day: 2017 September 23rd.

1 As free fair people of the (English language) Commonwealth Empire we humbly rely on the blessing of Almighty God (consequences from the laws of nature), and popular referendum of each participating (English language) Commonwealth Empire nation to agree to this one common FAIR CHARTER and Monarchy Crown [Queen Elizabeth II] with the English language with 42 character 42 phoneme phonetic alphabet, Border adjustment tax with 50% currency exodus tax area to be offsets from the exporters offset account to collect offsets at the rate of 25% of currency inflows into the national currency and nation from the exporters real exports, so reduce the tax on imports for this same exporter. Each English Language Commonwealth Empire member nations Parliament shall make subsequent legislative amendments (subject to adoption of this update by signature of the nations Prime Minister) to move towards having up to 100 pages of legislation to comply with this FAIR CHARTER of the (English language) Commonwealth Empire, subject to royal assent of this legislation by the English Monarchies Governor General for review by the Monarchy Crown [Queen Elizabeth II] within 1 year of passing the national parliament (also assent for each state parliament bill and local council chamber bill by the state governor).

Each member nation of the English Language Commonwealth Empire shall have a Governor General and a Prime Minister and own currency and border protection and anti-dumped product tariffs for quality control and protection of local industry. The English Language Commonwealth Empire FAIR CHARTER for nations who's majority fair citizens may join by random selection and vote as part of the Constitutional Court jury each month in conference from state (regardless of own constitutional arrangements); the nations of; The United States Of America with Canada (The American States); The United Kingdom with Scotland and Ireland (Britain); Australia with New Zealand, Tasmania and Antarctica (Australia); Israel (Izrael) with Jewish+Christian state and state for others, and The Commonwealth Of Independent States with Russia, Belarus, Ukraine, Poland, Kazakhstan, Kyrgyzstan, Moldova, Tajikistan, Azerbaijan, Uzbekistan and Armenia; Skandinave; Denmark, Norway, Denmark, Sweden, Finland to closest points between the white sea, lake Onega, and lake Ladoga, Iceland, Latvia, Estonia, Lithuania. Plus any additional associate nations who wish to use this fair FAIR CHARTER without constitution jury vote so not subverted demographically such as India, Turkmenistan, Philippines, Papua, Solomon Islands and Fiji. Each English Language Commonwealth Empire member nation shall include territorial seas and oceans to the mid-distance between the nations main contiguous land mass and the neighbouring nations main contiguous land mass. 40% of national revenue of the English Language Commonwealth Empire nations treasury shall be for national parliament treasurers budget allocations each of over 1% percentages of revenue cap for local, state and national minister spending from provider spending submissions to go to the national senate subject to the relevant minister. 40% of national revenue of the English Language Commonwealth Empire nations treasury shall be for 3 x 100gram best quality ration bars using local produce each day for each citizen including full and probationary citizens of the English Language Commonwealth Empire nation with ingredients as the health minister and the national parliament shall determine. 20% of national revenue of the English Language Commonwealth Empire nations treasury shall be for the English Language Commonwealth Empire Presidents broad military and foreign aid budget as the President shall prepare for approval by the English Language Commonwealth Empire citizens jury as may approve. The Presidents military and aid broad budget allocations each being over 1% of revenue for the English Language Commonwealth Empire national defence ministers and governor generals to sub-allocate. The governments of the independent nations of Papua and Mexico shall receive 10% of the English Language Commonwealth Empire military and foreign aid budget for nutritious 100gram long life ration bars (with choice of to contain temporary contraceptives and virile fertility versions) for all and also for water all as each Papuan and Mexican government shall approve. Plus only on Papuan and Mexican soil; open aid centres with aid centres for processing of blacks or illegals who have invaded our English Language Commonwealth Empire nations; for Papua and Mexico to receive and process those blacks or illegals who invaded so Papua and Mexico will keep own choice of more than 10% for more than 5 years after sending up to 90% of others elsewhere outside of our English Language Commonwealth Empire, We shall also protect Papua and Mexico people from invasion, as able. The English Language Commonwealth Empire nation government shall exile black or illegal fugitives who have invaded or who have failed DNA propensity (spit) test for residency. After prison for 1 month or over; all criminals including where local citizens or foreign shall return to nation of most ancestry or the nearest town to their place of birth or if an illegal or child of an illegal who has invaded to where of most percentage genetic ancestry of more than 500years for punishment including the death penalty. The democratic populist Prime Minister of each English Language Commonwealth Empire nation shall choose when to adopt this new more modern update of the FAIR CHARTER Of The

Commonwealth Empire for subsequent legislation to move towards compliance to.

2 English Commonwealth Empire Monarchy Crown [Queen Elizabeth II] powers to extend to the Crown's [Queen Elizabeth II] heirs on succession. The current English Commonwealth Empire Monarchy Sovereign Crown [Queen Elizabeth II] shall determine own heir and successor from own fair descendants and 10 closest relatives of over 50% British ancestry of more than 500 years, and subsequent heirs and successors lineage for update only by the current Monarchy Crown [Queen Elizabeth II], So to provide updates of own plans of succession in writing with the Monarchy Crown's [Queen Elizabeth II] own signature, to all Governor Generals of the English Commonwealth Empire to keep safe with terms for disclosure.

3 Proclamation of the FAIR CHARTER Of The Commonwealth Empire (Constitution): After submission of models from any fair full citizen of any English Commonwealth Empire member nation to the English Monarch and the nations Prime Minister, each month a voluntary 100 member citizens juries from each of the 10 states of all English Language Commonwealth Empire member nations shall vote together in an indicative plebiscite to rank submissions, the leading model shall then go to referendum of the same jury, each voluntary member on the Jury shall be by random selection from willing valid voters; to as Jurist cast valid votes which may be either way on the final submission to receive equal payment dividing 1% of the defence budget being 20% of English Language Commonwealth Empire revenue, So when passing then only come into law when the English Commonwealth Empire Crown [Queen Elizabeth II] will provide assent so become the current update of the FAIR CHARTER For Commonwealth Empire (Constitution); to which each member nations Prime Minister may decide when to adopt as the newer FAIR CHARTER Of The Commonwealth for the member nations subsequent legislation to move towards compliance to. The English Language Commonwealth Empire Monarchy Crown [Queen Elizabeth

II] may at any time suspend an update so as to require reversion so the for subsequent national legislation where using the model. The English Language Commonwealth Empire Monarch Crown [Queen Elizabeth II] may at any time determine a process for appointment and replacement of the Governor General of each English Language Commonwealth Empire member nation.

4 Commencement of membership as a English Language Commonwealth Empire nation: The nation shall come into membership of our English Language Commonwealth Empire of nations, subject to the current FAIR CHARTER Of The Commonwealth (Constitution) with effect, one month after successful referendum of all fair residents of the over 70% fair English language speaking nation. The Parliaments of several colonies may at any time vote as 10 states within the English Language Commonwealth Empire nation as a whole for as state to win approval be part of the Fair English Language Commonwealth Empire nation and subject to our new FAIR CHARTER Of The Commonwealth (Constitution).

5 Operation of the nations Constitution and laws: This; FAIR CHARTER Of The Commonwealth (Constitution), the Governor Generals military doctrine and all laws passing the national Parliament of the Commonwealth under the Prime Ministers choice of more recent update of the FAIR CHARTER Of The Commonwealth (Constitution) and with the nations Governor General assent subject to the English Language Commonwealth Empire Monarchy Crown [Queen Elizabeth II], shall apply to every part of the English Language Commonwealth Empire nation and shall be in effect on passing over all other laws and shall be binding on all courts, judges, religions and people of every State and seas and military ships and bases including embassies of the member nation subject to personal moral judgement and the current Prime Ministers signature as authorisation. Prior laws of any state shall continue to apply until new state legislation. The current English Language Commonwealth Empire Monarch Crown [Queen Elizabeth II] may grant case by case

Royal Pardon.

6 Repeal of Prior laws: Prior laws shall be void as much as were inconsistent with current newer laws subject to when able to pass new legislation to move towards compliance with the current FAIR CHARTER Of The Commonwealth as the Prime Ministers shall update to. Parliaments may repeal national legislation including international agreements and by replacement by subsequent national laws, subject to assent of the Monarchy Crown [Queen Elizabeth II].

7 The States shall mean each of the 10 states making up each English Language Commonwealth Empire member nation, each mainland state being within 10% equal (population x land area in hectares) then largest islands so each state to be the whole island.

8 The Governor General and Monarchy Crown [Queen Elizabeth II] may move and update (electoral and jurisdictional) boundaries; so add, remove and merge states so or our nation will have 10 states each with 10 local council areas, each of as equal as possible (population x land area in hectares), also considering natural boundaries such as of big islands, carrying capacity, natural species, pest control, climate and existing borders subject to the English Commonwealth Monarchy Crown [Queen Elizabeth II] royal assent.

9 General Structure of this FAIR CHARTER Of The Commonwealth; English Language Commonwealth Empire member nation governance shall be as follows:

Chapter I—The Federal Parliament

Part I—General

1 Legislative power: National legislative power shall reside with the Federal Parliament, which shall consist of Fair populist will, The Prime Minister ministers, the House of Representatives, the Senate, the Governor General and the English Commonwealth Monarchy Crown [Queen Elizabeth II].

2 Governor General: The English Language Commonwealth Empire Monarchy Crown [Queen Elizabeth II] shall determine and update a process for the appointment and replacement of each English

Commonwealth member nations Governor General and deputies and state Governors which the Crown [Queen Elizabeth II] may replace at any time by proclamation to the world and together shall determine assent of legislation passing the Federal Parliament, Plus confirm the coalition to be the government and the Prime Minister and ministry to present legislation and budget in the House of Representatives, The Prime Minister and Prime Ministers choice of Treasurer (subject to Royal assent) may only be from members having valid current election to the House of Representatives. Governor General assent is subject to the current English Language Commonwealth Empire fair Crown [Queen Elizabeth II] will of veto within one year of assent. The Governor General shall have such powers such as to appoint Military and Emergency services personnel and Replace government personnel (including where in office by election) to stand in (subject to performance and endurance) to the end of of the term at the next general election, with contracts terms of up to 5 years, subject to directions and law exemptions as the current English Language Commonwealth Empire Majesty fair Crown [Queen Elizabeth II] will assign and update.

[Crown [Queen Elizabeth II] Decree: Appointment of the Governor General shall be populist election by fair full citizens born in our nation, mothers shall vote for own children until ready to lodge own vote. Paper registration and postal ballot shall require ID with photo from post office, bill showing current address and for homeless post office may photograph, assess accent and eligibility and stamp, Voters able to confirm own vote online. Registration and update of registration shall require photo at post office. Excluding people of dark complexion, public servants, migrants or criminals having been in our prisons for over 1 month.]

3 Royal Estate Funding: 20% of government revenue of the Commonwealth nation shall be for the English Commonwealth military and aid budget for the Commonwealth nations Governor General to keep and spend within the same Commonwealth nation

from which 1% shall be for the Royal Estate to pay for upkeep of Royal Estate properties and staff, the salaries of the Commonwealth nations Governor General, State Governors, Prime Minister, Ministers and replacements who all may reside in Royal Estate properties and receive no pay from the Commonwealth nations government and political party budgets or be bribed during term/s of administration. Royal Estate income, properties and inheritance shall be tax free subject to 50% currency exodus tax if money taken out of the Fair English Commonwealth. Also 1% from which shall be for housing on the royal estate for descendants of fallen fair patriots who have died in action defending our commonwealth nation and justice and of siblings.

4 Provision for the Governor General: The Monarchy Crown [Queen Elizabeth II] shall determine the salary of a Governor General shall only be from the Royal Estate and be as the Crown [Queen Elizabeth II] shall determine prior to appointment and not alter during all terms in office as Governor General.

5 Sessions of Parliament, Prorogation and dissolution: The Governor General may determine times for holding the sessions of the Parliament, and may at any time by proclamation to the people to at which completion prorogue the Federal Parliament law making and dissolve the House of Representatives and Senate and reset all standing votes to recast on and from the election day on the 10th Sunday after proclamation with a maximum term as the Federal Parliament shall determine. Summoning Parliament; After any general election in the Fair English Language Commonwealth Empire Nation the Governor General shall summon the Federal Parliament to meet and by default thirty days after the day the people in the main vote (after referendum to establishment the nation as a Fair English Commonwealth member nation by default after six months).

6 Minimum sitting session of Parliament and Local council assemblies: Members of Parliament shall do a minimum of a 40 hour week (Monday to Friday) sitting every 3 months (for ordinary

members this may be by tele-conferance and tele-vote with video monitor in the members place and speaker control of hearing of the members microphone). The Prime Minister, Premier and Mayor for the assembly may determine extra sittings and extensions. The Governor General may also have an assembly sit or end sitting extensions.

Part II—The House of Representatives

7 the House of Representatives shall be two hundred members of the house; being one female and one male from each of the one hundred local council electorates; being ten local council areas in each of the ten states of the Commonwealth Empire nation. For each of the ten local councils in each of ten states of the Commonwealth Empire nation; Each of the twenty members of the local council by populist election to the local council shall have five equal value votes to elect one female member and five equal value votes to elect one male to the national House Of Representatives lower first house from the ten male candidates and ten female candidates, being one male candidate and one female candidate from each of the ten largest parties by membership in the local council area branch. Also for the state lower house each Local Council shall elect five men and five women from the five male and five female candidates from each of the top ten parties by membership in the local council area branch who reside in the electorate. With the candidates from fifty percent of party members born in the local council area and living in the state the longest including all lineages in the last one hundred years who attend the pre selection to be on the same Sunday each year. The Governor General shall direct and budget the royal electoral boundaries commission to draw state boundaries and the state Governor the local council boundaries including to be as electorates so each has as near as possible the same (population x land area in hectares) and so biggest islands are a electorate. Subject to assent of the state Governor and the Monarchy Crown [Queen Elizabeth II].

8 Alteration of number of members: Subject to the Commonwealth

FAIR CHARTER the national Parliaments may draft proposals to update the number of the members of the House of Representatives subject to the more up to date valid FAIR CHARTER For Fair Empire the Prime Minister chooses to update to (after approval by referendum of the English Language Commonwealth Empire Constitutional Court Jury and Monarchy Crown [Queen Elizabeth II])

9 Local council areas as local council and house of representatives electorate and jurisdictional divisions: The Governor General shall direct state Governors and fund the royal electoral boundaries commission to determine boundaries in each of the 10 states of the 10 local council areas to also the be 10 electoral divisions in each of the 10 states in the Commonwealth member nation each local council shall have within 10% equal (population x land area in hectares). On the Prime Minister updating to a more current FAIR CHARTER For Fair Empire the state Governor shall merge and divide prior local council (electoral) boundaries to comply with this new FAIR CHARTER For Fair Empire, subject to assent by the Governor General and the Monarchy the Crown [Queen Elizabeth II]assent.

10 Prior laws in relation to qualification of House Of Representatives electors: Local laws relating to qualification of electors shall remain in force until the Federal Parliament update legislation and until update of the national legislation to comply with the Prime Ministers choice of more recent update to the Fair English Language Commonwealth Empire FAIR CHARTER subject to royal assent of the Crown [Queen Elizabeth II]. The laws relating to elections to the lower house of the national parliament shall, as be nearly as practicable, apply to elections in the 10 state lower houses.

11 Voting for legislation and budget in the House of Representatives: A majority of votes being 126+ members including the speaker where equal shall determine motions in the House of Representatives. The speaker shall only vote where the numbers for and against an bill are equal, and then the speaker shall cast a vote to determine the result. The chamber may only update regulation as put by the minister and

after 50%+ and more of the members of the ruling Government coalition in the House of Representatives vote to do, undo, reform and redo the regulation of up to 1 A4 page of normal text. For a over all total of up to 100 pages of regulation of the Parliament in addition to up to 100 pages of total legislation including; legislation, the national Treasurers broad national budget and the Presidents English Language Commonwealth Empire broad defence budget.

Part III—The Senate

12 The senate: The senate shall be 200 lord senators; 10 senators from each state shall be female and 10 male; from each of the 10 States in the Commonwealth nation, with gender specific election of 100 senators every 2 ycars general election by appointment by direct election by the people of the State as one electorate so as to comply with the Prime Ministers choice of valid Fair English Language Commonwealth Empire FAIR CHARTER update. General election of members of house and senators of the gender shall be concurrent with this term subject to confirmation and assent of the State Governor the Governor General who may also appoint temporary replacements.

13 Election of senators from each state senate; To one year into the term for each of the top 10 parties by membership number only of the one party from full citizens may nominate for pre selection after 20 years probationary citizenship and 100 years own and ancestral full citizenship adding together all full citizen ancestors in the last 100years and be of 50% of members with longest membership only with the one state branch of the party and living within the state. So from the parties members who are full citizens after 20 years probationary citizenship and 100 years own and ancestral full citizenship adding together all full citizen ancestors in the last 100years, from which 50% with longest own and ancestral (adding together all lineages) membership of only the state branch of the party shall by postal vote pre-select 10 candidates for to be senate candidates for party so go on the state postal ballot paper. General election standing votes shall continue to be valid until replacement or

death or no longer a valid voter. If the candidacy was withdrawn standing votes for remaining candidates remain valid until update.

14 Method of election of senators; Voting shall be for from 100 senate candidates in the state electorate of the citizen valid voters birth. The valid electors where born and living in the state shall each cast and number 10 same value postal standing votes for separate valid candidates plus up to 2 spare votes for any of the 100 valid senate candidates of the gender of the state. Voters shall be able to verify own standing votes online after cast by postal ballot and counting.

15 Permanent vacancy by notification, vacancy, absence, crimes or illness: Whenever a permanent vacancy happens in the Senate as the Governor General shall determine. Such as one of the Speaker and deputy speakers of the senate notify the Governor General. The replacement may be next in line currently qualifying candidate by votes from the ex-senators party on the the ballot paper for the state from the general election as the replacement, if none the Governor General may determine a replacement. For up to the remainder of the 3 year term of the Senate and then subject to election subject to assent from the Governor of the State to have 10 session sitting days to first attend a session sitting as a Senator.

16 Voting in the Senate: Bills in the Senate shall require 150+ votes for the bill of more than 240 Senators in the Senate chamber. The Speaker may only vote on determine bills otherwise failed having equal votes for and against. After 6 months and a vote each month in the senate the final bill before the Senate after the final bill passes the House Of Representatives; the Prime Minister may have a joint sitting of both houses of parliament to require a simple majority of 201 members from the house and the senator voting from own chamber then adding the votes of both chambers together.

Part IV—Both Houses of the the national and state parliaments and for local council chambers.

17 Right of electors of States: All valid voters may cast a vote for candidates to be the members of the local council in the local council

area of the voters birth (for to elect members of lower first house in the state and the national parliament) and for candidates in the state electoral area of the voters birth (for election of the senate). No law or person may prevent a valid voter from voting as the Prime Ministers Commonwealth FAIR CHARTER update on enactment on these law determines. Disqualification of dark complexion or criminal propensity races or of terrorist religions: All persons of any dark complexion or criminal propensity race or terrorist religion are disqualified from voting and shall not be counted in election.

18 Qualifications of voters and candidates and 20 members (10 male and 10 female) of each of the 100 local councils and the 200 members (100 male and 100 female) of the national house of representatives and the 200 (100 male and 100 female) senators of the national senate and members of political parties and common public servants and of 100 members of 10 state lower houses and 100 jurists of the 10 state upper houses (forming parts of the citizens council English Language Commonwealth Empire constitutional court jury): When the Federal Parliament updates national legislation to comply with the Prime Ministers choice of this more recent Commonwealth FAIR CHARTER the qualifications shall be as follows: The voters, candidate and members must be the full age of twenty years, and must be born in the electorate to run for and represent, have more than 100 years ancestral (adding together lineages) citizenship in last 200 years with none of black complexion and have productive contribution to the English Language Commonwealth Empire nation. Plus not be of an illegal terrorist religion. Plus not been a bankrupted or addicted or convicted to prison for 1 or more years (subject to acquittals and Royal pardons) and protect the productive citizens of the English Language Commonwealth Empire nation. To gain election for a total of terms adding up to 10 years and then until the next general election subject to replacement at any time by standing vote of the electorate. Disqualification: Any person who; (i) has been born, under any allegiance, obedience, or adherence to a foreign power or any terrorist

religion or entitled to the rights or privileges of any foreign power; or (ii) has been a traitor to the fair people of the Commonwealth Empire nation, or who has had a genetic propensity to have done savage or deviant crimes. (iii) has been bankrupted; or (iv) has bribed or taken bribes particularly if was paid or promised payment from foreigners while in office or extorted pay for any populis service job such by associating with in a union while a populis servant; or (v) has had any profit from dealings with any Government of more than the Commonwealth nations GDP / population [$75,000] other than welfare common to all citizens and equal pay from surplus as normal public service volunteer plus the Governor General may provide a bonus to ministers of government by election. A Governor Generals royal court shall determine cases of who shall have disqualification of voting, being a candidate, being chosen or of sitting as any member of any position in any public service including by election in the English Commonwealth. Legal pay shall include Equal welfare for productive if poor in assets where a born citizens and a full citizen after 20 years probationary citizenship, Plus populis service bonus being equal portions of 40% of the budget surplus over 52 weeks for each hour of populis servants active work, 10% of the surplus for parties in proportion to number of representatives having election, 50% of the budget surplus for to build national socialist housing. Plus pay from the Monarchy Crown [Queen Elizabeth II]through the Governor General for services such as to replace personnel and for some military personnel, Plus special reward for prosecuting criminals, Plus any pay for independent private enterprise including wages and income from investments subject to open disclosure on own web-site at bottom of home page. The Monarchy shall not have only have income as the Commonwealth nations Governor Generals NATO military budget shall disclose. Military the Commonwealth nation may invite may also have official income from own country but may not take bribes. People of dark complexion or of criminal propensities shall determine and enforce own customary rights in native title areas and prison islands subject to Police self defence and Military national defence.

19 Practice and conduct of elections; Electors (voters) must present valid proof of identity with photo to local post office to lodge votes. The national Parliament of the English Language Commonwealth nation may make sub-laws in relation to election and replacement of senators so the method shall be uniform for all of the 10 states. Subject to these laws, the state parliament may make sub-laws in relation to conduct of election of senators for that State. Times and places: The elector put a postal ballot with state senators and local council members sections) into an official official voting mail box at a local post office after proving identity with official photo ID, remote elector voters may post ballot with proof of identity using any post box. To when arrive at the state Governor Generals vote counting centre/s be subject to manual count by each the Governor Generals official counters then each of the 10 parties official counters in turn with over watch by the Governor Generals official scrutineers. Local Council may submit locations for extra vote box with number and lock for the Local Council to collect and deliver to post office to account for and submit as the state Governor shall determine.

20 Compulsory voting; All fair free private good full citizens valid electors from 20 years shall vote including for females valid voters for valid birth children from birth to 20 years of age, children who are valid voters from 10 years of age may voluntarily register and cast own voluntary vote. When over the age of 20 years fine of 1% of income from manual productivity until lodging valid standing votes, except convicts or addicts and members of official ministers public service including NATO and by election shall have cancellation of standing votes so so as to have populist democratic election not totalitarian self election. For children the mother and guardian (not government) shall cast votes for each eligible child until 10 years of age and then until the child is ready to register to vote and cast own vote. Valid voters may update standing paper secret ballet postal votes

at any time (with online verification and posting out of new ballot for next update at any time).

21 Oath or affirmation of allegiance: Every senator and every member of the House of Representatives and every member of a local council, shall before taking seat make and subscribe before the Commonwealth Monarchy Crown [Queen Elizabeth II]'s Governor General, an oath or affirmation of allegiance to the Commonwealth Crown [Queen Elizabeth II] and FAIR CHARTER in the form set forth by the Crown [Queen Elizabeth II].

22 Resignation of a member: A member may by address the Speaker of the chamber and present the Speaker with a written resignation, the relevant state Governor may accept a resignation letter for confirmation by phone call.

23 Writs for vacancies: If a vacancy happens in a chamber such as through was disqualified, resigned, ill, lazy, prisoned, or died, the relevant state Governor may issue the writ for the election of a new member within the next 30 days.

24 Writs for general election of the House of Representatives and Senate of the national Parliament: The Governor General in council with the Prime Minister may cause writs to issue for dates of an early general elections from 1 year after the last general election day and at a maximum 3 years after the last election day; for all members with immediate cancellation of all standing votes, then after one month valid voters then have one month to cast new standing votes for local council members and senate senators then one month to count and for the state Governor to confirm the states senate and local council members then one month for each of 100 local councils to convene and each elect a single male representative and a single female representative to the national house of representatives lower first houses and for the Governor General to determine the Governing coalition having 101+ valid members of the House Of Representatives. Within these four months the existing government shall remain and function normally if this has taken longer than four

weeks the existing opposition shall become the Government until the Governor General will determine the proper government, the maximum term of the opposition being 1 year then a new automatic general election. Subject to the Monarchy Crown [Queen Elizabeth II] determination of results.

25 Candidates may only run for and have election as member of only one seat at a time. A valid person may only have appointment to one house of Parliament.

26 Electors must register and update permanent address. Voting is compulsory for valid voters with fine of 4% of income while having failed to lodge valid vote except where incapacitated.

27 Those who have abused our fair races as citizens may not be a member of a political party. Blacks or convicts or foreign born may not be a member of a political party.

28 Vacancy on disqualification: If disqualification of any public servant including any member of parliament by Royal Court the place shall thereupon become vacant.

29 Penalty for sitting when disqualified: Any person subject to disqualification by Royal Court from sitting in a Parliament shall, for every day for which he has sit illegally, pay national an amount in national currency of GDP / population / 100 [$700] to any person who prove it in any local council court and a Royal Court for Governor General assent subject to repeal within 1 year by the English Commonwealth Monarchy Crown [Queen Elizabeth II].

30 Disputed elections: The Governor General's Royal Court may resolve disputed elections.

31 Allowance to members: Each populis servant including by election each to receive equal portion of 40% of the budget surplus for each active hour over 52 weeks after passing the budget. Parties shall receive a portion of 10% of the national budget in proportion to number of members having election.

32 Powers, privileges, rules and immunities of the parliament grounds: Shall update by the Prime Minister with Governor General

assent.

33 Absence of a speaker (chair of the chamber): After 5 minutes in a session sitting without a speaker in the speakers chair including any of the 3 deputies; the chamber may elect to approve a member by of the chamber to become the new speaker (chair) and appoint 3 deputies from members.

34 The Speaker (chair) of the chamber shall cease to hold this office if has ceased to be a member by populist and chamber election. The Governor General may also determine the senate replace and ban a member from being speaker of the chamber. The speaker of the chamber may also resign by verbal address to the chamber and also by writing to the Governor General with verbal confirmation such as by phone.

35 Speakers (chairs) rules and orders for the chamber: The speaker of each chamber of an assembly of public servants having election shall be within I week of the speaker setting new precedence update the powers, privileges, rules and immunities of the members of the chamber, the mode in which its powers, privileges, and immunities may be exercised and upheld subject to Royal (Governor General) veto. Also Speakers may use rules of any English Commonwealth parliament chamber such as of the Housed of Commons of the national Parliament of the United Kingdom.

36 Valid absence from the senator: Shall include for family responsibilities and official business. The senator may lodge written request for temporary absence and name a valid proxy member from the same chamber, and state as temporary replacement for up to 2 months absence with the Governor General for approval stamp and signature then confirmation such as by phone. So then be the temporary proxy replacement. Members may also attend from a local electoral office using tele conferencing with pop up monitor in place in chamber, microphone line into speaker (chairs) control panel screen, Plus with electronic vote with bio-metric such as face recognition.

37 Application of existing laws: Existing laws in relation to the chamber shall apply until update of the Commonwealth nations constitutions to comply with the Prime Ministers choice of Commonwealth FAIR CHARTER model when this update.

38 Failed attendance of members to the chamber: The chamber may proceed with business even if members have failed to arrive for the session from 10am on session days until adjournment by more than 60% of attending members by vote after the ringing of the signal bells with green light for House of Representatives and red light for Senate and signal bell throughout the Federal Parliament for 5 minutes or also after the leader in the chamber of the Prime Ministers Government calls for adjournment.

39 Vacancy by absence: If the place of the member, the members choice of a fellow member of the chamber as proxy and a Governor General stand in appointee has been vacant for 50% of the last 10 sitting days, the Governor General shall choose a replacement until return of the member until the next election such as a By-election and the General-Election. (an ordinary member may also attend the chamber by tele conference and tele vote)

40 Issue of writs: The Governor General shall issue writs for the General Election for the parliaments and local councils chambers at the same time.

41 Parliament and local council members terms: Each term of the Senate and Senators shall be for up to 3 years together with the House of Representatives. Each senator has a maximum duration as a senator of 10 yeas plus to the next general election.

42 Each hour of debate shall alternate between subject of a member of the government in full rotation and member of the opposition in full rotation. The call shall go to a members on request having least speaking time in last week alternating the call between a government and opposition member.

43 Quorum: More than 20% of the members by election of the chamber must be in the chamber for a quorum so debate may proceed.

More than 240 valid members must be in the chamber for a valid vote after ringing signal bell with red light throughout the national parliament. Attendance of more members than who vote on the bill in the chamber within 1 month may have the chamber vote again on the bill.

44 Members of an an assembly by election may not mention any other nation or celebrate any other ethic nationality.

Part V—Powers of the National Parliament

45 Legislative powers of the national Federal Parliament: This Parliament shall, subject to this Constitution, have power to make laws for the peace, order, good and fair governance of the Commonwealth over:

(i)Additional taxation so as to be the same in all parts of the Commonwealth nation, with free trade among our 10 States;

(ii)Transaction taxes; 50% Border Adjustment Tax on all currencies exodus from the USA, Canada, UK, Australia, New Zealand, Antarctica, Ireland and Israel currencies zone (such as on shifted profits so avoided tax, foreign owners or to buy imported products) offset by 25% offset bounty subsidy for inflows from abroad into deposits in any of the nations 10 national official private banks in the nations official national currency. [for Australia into Australian dollars the nations legal currency] So as to have this one uniform 50% rate of currencies exodus tax and 25% bounty subsidy offset throughout the currencies zone of USA, Canada, UK, Australia, New Zealand, Antarctica, Ireland and Israel currency zone) [turbo charger: the amount of export revenue inflows 4+x cost of the offset bounty subsidy] for export of real products (once) for where over 50% of manufacture manual labour working hours of the product is within the zone member nation plus postage and delivery of up to 50% of the price, The exporter gaining these offsets in own bank account to access first to offset so deduct from currencies exodus tax bill to pay such as by additional payment and from the transaction its self. For collection by the payment system such as of banks to keep 1% of revenue. 10% tax on transactions with a foreign currency (of a nation outside the Fair English Language Commonwealth Empire) and with other digital currencies where from, to and in our English Commonwealth currencies zone. 1% electronic transaction tax (transactions to self are tax free) on each entity where between separate entities to, from and in our English Commonwealth currencies zone. 10% foreign currency tax (any transaction in our nation using foreign currency to buy something) or inter-currency transaction tax: tax on currency conversion in our nation (conversion of any currency into our national currency free of this tax). Each individual and each shop may own physical cash up to the value of (GDP divide by population then divide by 10) [$7,000]. Each individual and each physical shop may have up to 1 kilogram bullion. Transactions in physical cash shall be free of all taxes within the Fair English Language Commonwealth Empire nation including .999%+ silver (with matte gray oxidisation coating) as legal tender by oz weight. Merchants may round up cash payments and so keep change in line with visible merchant policy.

(iii)GDP divide by population then divide by 100 [AUD$700] per ton single rate bounty (quantitative easing subsidy) on food grown on dry nutritional proteins, amino-acids, vitamins, minerals, good fats and nutraceuticals content (not on simple sugars or bad fats content) of food grown and for consumption in the Fair English Language Commonwealth nation, Repayment penalty if wasted.

(iv)Product categories to have a 50% import duty (tariff) for which the Commonwealth nation can produce a replacement (not on individual foreign companies and products). Levy per kilogram on export of products sourced from living nature such as seafood and timber for seeding and replenishment of these species.

(v)For seller revenue of over GDP / population in last year; 10% all sales levy tithe for sellers choice of free teachers and 10% all sales levy for equal wages each hour for sellers choices of best 80% of manual labour hours with if poor in assets having the right to attend workplace for own choice of apprenticeship subject to ban by court if was criminal; For collection by the sales platform and bank with no taxes and levies. 30% levy on shares sales to go to the underlying business to prevent high frequency faked mania trading and have real investment;

(vi)Export royalties: GDP / population then / 2000 [$35] per ton royalty on general exports (for gas the weight as a liquid), plus GDP / population then / 100 [$700] per ton for natural forest sourced timber and wild ocean sourced sea life exports) to pay once (may come and go free after paying export royalty once). To be free; people and also luggage up to 10kg, plus free aid and means of transport and military. For fair states exporters to spend royalties to build power stations for base-load eternal electricity generation and for uninterrupted power supplies (batteries) including for small exporters with management by the seller platform. Where from native title territory dark state payment on the native title territory state border for equal distribution between all citizens of dark complexion residing in native title territory (state). Natural resource must be available for sale to the majority of local consumers in the fair Commonwealth nation at under half the price available to overseas (export) consumers (including cost of delivery).

(vii)1% wealth tax. For real property accumulating each year, paid if sold after dividing by contiguous area in hectares (not paid on inheritance unless sold). The eldest natural child in turn to inherit own choice of contiguous real estate property including productive inputs, furniture and machinery assets such as for agriculture tax free up to the price of GDP divide by population then multiple by 100 [$7m] (for each natural child). Financial type investments are subject to .1% tax each month, for shares this shall be by issue of shares to treasury on behalf of the company by the exchange of this percentage of total shares in existence including as company options. Additional personal and family food, goods, vehicles and furniture of the higher of normal new cost price and current sell-able price have the first GDP divide by population then multiply by number of resident natural children to age 25 years) [$70,000x number of resident children] free of tax, for the excess to pay a 10% wealth tax every 10 years. Property and assets of charities having approval of the local council are free of wealth tax. Gifts of a value of GDP/population [$70,000] each year (accumulating) such as including inheritance to be tax free. Additional gifts and inheritances are subject to 50% tax. 5% levy each year for all citizens over 50 years of age on all wealth over national GDP for year to divide by population [aud$70,000] to pay in cash equally between natural children of any age plus may add additional children to age of 20 years of age tax free into the own emergency savings account of each child.

(viii) Loans taxes; 1% tax each year on all financial loans to apply to all financial lenders.

(ix) For foreigners living overseas; vacant bedroom tax of 1% of the property price each month to then divide by number of potential bedrooms so determine tax for each potential bedroom.

(x) Customs, quarantine, inoculation and biological pest elimination. Navigation tools, traffic control, lighthouses, lightships, beacons and buoys. Mapping, documentation and reporting of astronomical, meteorological and scientific observations;

(xi) Conservation of islands and seas within the national territorial waters (mid distance between own main-land area and the main land area of neighbouring nations);

(xii) Currencies, finance, banking, equal self adding voucher card welfare, coinage, money supply, interest rate policy and transactions within the Commonwealth nation. To encourage savings rather than insurance; 10 local banks shall manage all accounts as units in the banks 1 shares fund: all these Savings including mandatory emergency savings accounts and Super accounts shall invest 100% in local (within own Fair Commonwealth nation not in foreign nations) infrastructure; 50% as shares and 50% as own build rental housing.

(xiii) Communications. (People shall have the right to tell and know the truth subject to sexual privacy and money account security, Plus military action secrecy for 1 year), Spectrum, Television and radio may only broadcast voices, songs and sounds of fair complexion people, policy, nature, true images, science, design and events, and silent video of black or criminal activities, Television may only show sport with racist white power music but may not broadcast any sounds or voices of or about sport (such as on radio). Fiction and degenerate music shall Digital Rights Management to prevent copy, play or broadcast without permission of and payment to the creators, Racist white power music which shall be free to copy, broadcast, stream and play. Video security surveillance shall monitor and record silent video of all public places to catch crime including public toilets. Reverse or virtual images, animation or deviant art, Voices, sounds, songs, messages or art of homosexuals, black people or of illegal terrorist religions may not be broadcast, heard, seen or published except as imposed in close physical proximity, from which you may defend self, discourage, vilify, ignore and leave. Government must tell the truth and may not directly pay for media, The maximum revenue in last year of a media maker organisation and teacher such as of video channel and software shall be GDP to divide by population to then multiply by 100 [$7million], the surplus to donate to the media makers choice of media makers and teachers under this limit (separate from private broadcast infrastructure provider such as of satellites who may have any revenue). All media must be by individuals, charities and private businesses, The nation may only own some broadcast infrastructure such as towers, cables and data centre buildings for sharing with a board of 10 being 1 director from each of the 10 biggest parties by adding together current votes of fair full citizens at national, state and local government elections. Channel receiving most levy sponsorship in last month such as from levy on sales for the business choice of educational video channel to be broadcast on the relevant spectrum.

RADIO SPECTRUM: All broadcast spectrum is free to 10 private media corporations having approval of the national business council and receiving most media levy sponsorship or mobile Internet spectrum and fibre 1/10 bandwidth free to 10 telecommunications company connecting most {actual 25mbps+} broadband users. Government may not sell or charge rent for spectrum. As set by the national parliament {Device transmitting under 100Milliwatt may use any spectrum without limit, restriction or cost, up to 10MHz per user allowing devices to switch to unused frequencies, Except may not use GPS, radar, navigation, emergency, and missile guidance spectrum up to 100mhz. Radio Quiet Zone: a radius of {} shall have no radio emissions except in emergencies for radio telescope.

*25khz from 0khz to 25khz military submarine communications.

*25khz from 25khz to 50khz positioning system.

*25khz from 50khz to 100khz over the horizon radar.

*400khz from 100khz to 500khz Point of sale automatic teller banking transaction and payment with encryption, (40channels x 10khz) Such as by satellite and by point to point tower. Traffic signal control, and satellite clock and wrist-watch time synchronisation signal. Automatic satellite and tower ship and aircraft location reporting and navigation information system and emergency locator beacon satellite. Remote smart meter reading, to use mobile phone spectrum where able.

*29.5mhz from 500khz to 30mhz; Multiuse as military shall require such as for drones then as local council shall configure and transmit configuration to ham transceiver visual channel labels on transceiver display and regulate maximum power and channel width (1khz to 20khz). With higher power channels at lower frequencies from 1watt to 300watts. Channels for data such as transceiver position and call sign and packet radio internet, Drones, Open business, emergency services and citizens bands push to talk open channels (not jammed or messed up with encrypted traffic noise).

*20mhz from 30mhz to 50mhz carrier point to point wireless dish dynamic spectrum. For top 100 national backbone network provider carrier; for connection of low latency remote mobile device towers for mainly voice calls up to 5mbps speed cap to spread bandwidth to more users, so to use satellite dish for more latency tolerant wireless broadband. All of this spectrum is available to each of these carrier tower provider. Multiple user dynamic spectrum bandwidth channels, so fit as many users as each will get 5mbps. Carrier to use minimum required power per dynamic channel to provide good low latency voice connection by minimum power up to 100watts (Internet to use satellites as can tolerate longer latency).

*100mhz from 50mhz to 150mhz Open free {5G} cellular wi-fi dynamic spectrum (band 1) only for longest range connections up to 10mbps cap to spread bandwidth better to all users; Free open equal sharing of long range open spectrum wireless as required of standards set by the national parliament. Multiple user dynamic spectrum bandwidth channels, so fit as many users as each will get 5mbps with cap of 10mbps, With users to output just enough power for good voice connection of devices at more than 5mbps: Anyone may use and provide open spectrum wireless access using own backbone network connection and only for free. People may share open spectrum wireless passwords in exchange for roaming use of open spectrum wireless access. 1% of national budget for free open all areas hot-spots including Drones, lamp lamp posts, stadiums, schools, universities, hospitals, nursing homes, clinics, digital library charities, sports facilities, swimming pools, beaches, zoos, parks, conservation areas, tourist attractions, theatres, entertainment facilities, night clubs, shopping centres, malls, shops, restaurants, factories, city multi story buildings, churches, and community centres, Such as for owners, tenants, visitors, customers, workers, passengers, patients and students. Including for voip video phone calls. The free access point provider paying for routers, amplifier, antenna, and backbone network access such as by fibre. Devices do not have to use the same access method to receive and send access to network. Access point senders able to have many users on each dynamic channel. Maximum power being minimum required to have good connection with maximum number of devices so able to provide 5mbps up to 100watts/channel. Wireless router to selection 3 last channels, then drop channel with lowest speed (most interference) and replace with channel for which having lowest signal level (not recently failed channels) for minimum interference. Also 2% of national budget for remote fibre backbone network with 10 {[Internet] standard as set by the national parliament} network fibres plus 10 cable TV fibres. With wireless towers for local connection for mobile phone and broadband. Each network fibre and each TV fibre for the network cable builder company from more than 10 having approval of the state parliament who lay most 20+ fibre backbone in the nation to charge only for fibre backbone network access (including for open wireless network access). So users able to change channels within 1 second. Tenant and property owners at the location may get free fibre network access and pay TV for allowing use of yard and roof for free wireless access services tower and antenna base station hub with eternal generator and battery, for the hub owner to provide open wireless network access to neighbours and visitors to pay just for fibre network access from own choice from the 10 fibre network builder. All users may live bid per megabyte for backbone fibre access for wireless with commercial satellite fall-back where available if wireless network access transfer rate has fallen a mega bits per second level set by the user. Devices must have automatic power control to transmit minimum required variable power output to only transmit minimum wireless signal power required by the user to connect and use device successfully. Peer to peer user and provider may also use point to point parabolic dish to collect and send signal with motor to auto focus such as to connect with neighbours. Also for free wireless open channel voice and peer to peer web tiles for services and people profiles in local proximity tiles subject to user filter for mobile phone and stationary vehicle. Maximum power minimum required to connect full screen of tiles to 100watts. Sender user may set password to only sent tiles and open voice channel to people in proximity having the same password.

Such as for sending personal emergency alerts. Also for Internet Of Things processing of data (may also use mobile phone/device spectrum): Smart tags, meters and sensors, Cordless phones, headphones and microphone, Remote control, Smart appliances, Traffic lights, signs and traffic alerts for vehicle AI, cameras, security sensors, speakers, home and industry equipment control systems, Toys, Vehicle to vehicle communications, Peer to peer browser showing tiles in order of proximity of devices self hosting. With and without passwords. Up to 500milliwatts/channel home devices, up to 5watts/channel outdoor device, up to 50watts/channel. Auto vacant channel switching.

*100mhz from 150mhz to 250mhz (100channels x 1mhz) for 100 {[DAB+] standard as set by the national parliament} satellite and tower digital radio stations including for backup. Each of stations for the private media corporations having approval of a member of the national parliament to receive most sponsorship from levy on sales for the income earners choice of private media corporation for free to air free commercials media. All English language. {1-World economics and policy article reading service. 2-recital of all 1764 combinations of the 42x42 letter phonetic alphabet brain exercise. 3-Christian and Jewish music radio. 4-Live national talk-back, 5-Crime, police, criminal law and trials radio. 6-emergency services: auto switch with manual over-ride to broadcast emergency services control centre where having most communications. 7-Weather radio. 8-Off grid living article reading service. 9-Natural cycles and prophecy. 10-Environmental radio. 11-Secrets disclosure and conspiracy. 12-Pets and animal welfare radio. 13-Nutritional medicine article reading radio. 14-Exercise and fitness radio. 15-Celebrity gossip radio. 16-Product review radio (selection not for payment of money). 17-Science and technology article reading service. 18-Shopping (paid advertisements) radio. 19-Criminal law and courts radio. 20-Fair instrumental music. 21-Japan news and programs in English. 22-Breakthrough constant free energy, time travel, chronovision, teleportation and anti-gravity technology. 23-Farm journal article reading service and news, 24-Computer and communications article reading service. 25-Racist white (fair complexion) pride and empowerment music with ~50% of each gender, 26-Populist nationalist music from fair musicians born in, ancestry and recording from the same Fair English Language Commonwealth Empire nation ~50% from each gender, 27-National news. 28-International news from local perspective, 29-British news and non fiction programs in English, 30-European, Scandinavian and Russian news and programs in English, 31-Israel news and programs in English, 32-Irish news and programs in English. 33-Canadian news and programs in English. 34-New Zealand news and programs in English. 35-USA news and programs in English. 36-China region news and programs in English. 37-Australian news and programs in English. 3-Local industry news and programs in English. 39-Fair citizens interests. 40-National parliament: house of representatives male members and press conference radio. 41-Australian national parliament: senate chamber female senators and press conference radio. 42-Military, police and emergency services. 43-Canada news and programs in English. 44-European parliament, news and press conference radio, 45-55State parliaments and local council chamber and press conference radio, 56-{for the national parliament to decide} 57-{for the national parliament to decide}. 58-UFOs and extra terrestrial affairs articles and interviews. 59-War or disaster history. 60-Shares investment news and article reading service. 60-100 Live country and regional affairs, news and talk stations from 4 largest local council areas from the 10 in each state.} Spectrum for satellite: No junk, free to air TV: All channels must be non fiction, non cartoon or computer graphics (except numbers and alphabet), English language, all sounds and art must be of people having fair complexion and not degenerate violent savagery voices and culture of black complexion people. No homosexual propaganda. Paid advertisement only product placement and taking up to 50% of screen so able to press key on remote to hear advertising over normal programming. Faber network cable may have any (junk) content.

*75mhz from 250mhz to 325mhz (10channels x 10mhz)

Day: (9am to 5pm) 10 child education television all English channels for pay television satellite owners to broadcast. With backup hill top tower transmitters. 10 age levels child education channels. For the channel receiving most sponsorship from levy on business sales revenue for educational television channels and videos to host on {[YouTube] video host/s as set by the national parliament}. No cartoons.

Night: (5pm to 9am) 10 high definition all English television channels for the private charity of the particular speciality receiving most from 10% levy on income to manage using private educational television satellite owner as the national government will choose and commission. With optional text article selection from part of screen. All English: 1-News, protests, breakthroughs, politics, discoveries, events, justice, disasters, accidents, aid, rescue, sports highlights, weather from the local nation perspective. 2-Silent sport with racist white power music, 3-Food, travel, tourism, food gardening, farming, nutritional and fitness, 4-Nature documentary, anatomy, biology, natural sciences, health, 5-Technical science and technology: breakthroughs news and documentaries, information technology, genetics, materials, nutritional medicines, anti-gravity, energy, space, interstellar travel, 6-Current affairs, policy, shares, economic indicators, investment and finance, discussion in detail, news conferences, media presentations, parliament highlights, 7-Advertisements channel with sound as on up to 50% of screen on all channels with optional mute on remote control, 8Home making, renovation, building, real estate, furniture, antiques,, 9-Gossip, celebrity, performing arts, fashion, modelling, fertility, psychology, relationships, nudity, romance, beauty, reality, lifestyle, games, comedy and entertainment, 10-Data-cast teletext channel such as of subscribers [Twitter] messages only to the subscriber and message service account holder.

*75mhz from 325mhz to 400mhz (10channels x 7.5mhz)

Day: (9am to 5pm) 10 channels high definition research female university television all English channels for private pay television satellite owner to broadcast the relevant {[YouTube] online video libraries having approval of the national parliament} channel receiving most sponsorship from levy sales for free online educational video channels and video: 1-Nursing, healing. 2-Music for racist fair people empowerment. 3-Merchant shop keeping. 4-Child care and education. 5-Fertility and child birth. 6-Home keeping and budget management. 7-Nutrition, food preparation and service. 8-Welfare and charity. 9-Manufacturing and hand craft. 10-Hygiene and infection control.

Night: (5pm to 9am) Satellite internet with block on fictional video so not jammed.

*75mhz from 400mhz to 475mhz (10channels x 7.5mhz)

Day: (9am to 5pm) 10 channels high definition research male university television channels for private pay television satellite owner to broadcast the relevant {[YouTube] online video libraries having approval of the national parliament} channel receiving most sponsorship from levy sales for free online educational video channels and video: All English: 1- Agriculture,- Food, nutritional supplements, diet, tourism, crops, seeding timing, harvest timing, agricultural machinery mechanics and service, fencing, water supply, timber, paper, leather and natural textiles, (Best crop selection research focus), 2-Engineering,- metal casting, milling, welding, coatings, 3D printing, ceramics, composites, plastics, robotics, machine tools, kiln work, chemistry and materials science, (Material science + Product design research focus), 3-Computing, networks, video displays and audio: networks, computers, electronics, microchips manufacture, satellites, spectrum, television, audio, chronovision, wireless Internet communications, (Web-page design, Quantum computing + Crystal power focus), 4-Resources: geology, minerals exploration, excavation, explosives, mining machinery, ore processing, smelting, environment protection, water works, sewage, (Geology mapping focus), 5-Construction: concrete slab work, tile and brick laying, glass work, sheds and roof work, plumbing and bathrooms, tunnelling, roads, bridging, kitchens, carpets, curtains, furniture and carpentry (Construction planning+design research focus), 6-Health: Fertility, genetics, dentistry, infections, trauma, cancer, medical research, organ failure, addiction, allergies, diabetes, immunology, hygiene, poisons, ambulance paramedics, (Nutrition medicine research focus), 7-Genetics, Crop, Pest or black race specific contraceptive infections, Human genetics. (Genetics focus) 8-Finance: Business, administration, retail, economics, banking, shares analysis, investment, (Investment audit research focus), 9-Transport and robotics,- anti-gravity, interstellar travel, teleportation, robot vehicles, robotics, space probe exploration, satellites, time travel, driving, trucking, shipping, railways, aviation, packaging, logistics, customisation, repair, mechanics, packaging, minerals transport, space communications, and space telescopes, cognitive programming (Transport engineering focus), 10- Policy: Law, media, child care, education, music, colour, alphabet, naming, constitution, democracy (Constitution design research focus).

 Night: (5pm to 9am) Satellite internet with block on fictional video so not jammed.

*25mhz from 475mhz to 500mhz open license spectrum any use to 10 watts.

*3ghz from 500mhz to 3.5ghz for (300 channels x 10mhz with spectrum at 2.45ghz for microwave oven); Free open less than 1millisecond latency {5G} cellular wi-fi (band 2) mobile device dynamic spectrum. Selection of 4-10 last channels to requirements, then dropping of channel with lowest speed (most interference) and replacement with channel having lowest signal strength for minimum interference) for ground tower, lamp posts, and on roof wireless Internet. {[5G using Artemis pCell pre processing signal focusing technology] standard as set by the national parliament} [With 100 pCell (devices) per 10 pWave (antenna) cell using just 5mhz: 3ghz would provide much more network capacity than we all could possibly use so we might as well use extra surplus spectrum for additional uses] To user own choice of any backbone network provider such as a neighbour with optical fibre. The user and provider may have a billing system, With use device able to switch instantly to backbone network provider with cheapest backbone network rates including optical fibre and satellite. Multiple small cell local wireless micro-node signal boxes (such as in secure safe off road cabinet on royal estate national socialist housing land, so not going to be hit by a car) also for drones, hilltop towers and satellite. For mobile devices with internal antenna 10 centimetres or less in length with local cell maximum power 20watts/channel, with drones, hilltop towers and satellites maximum power 100watts/channel. *Spectrum at 1.57542ghz and 1.2276ghz for global positioning system.

*500mhz from 3.5ghz to 4ghz high power radar spectrum.

*6ghz spectrum from 4ghz to 10ghz for satellite up-links spectrum in proportion to down-link spectrum allocation.

*20ghz spectrum from 10ghz to 30ghz. Radar.

*50ghz spectrum from 30ghz to 80ghz free open radar spectrum for vehicle such as for taxi and drone auto pilot self navigation mapping. To 10watts emitter. Subject to local council restrictions.

*20ghz spectrum from 80ghz to 100ghz Free open use spectrum such as for spectrum hopping wireless local wireless device to screen video, data and audio links subject to local council and federal minister restrictions. Up to 100mhz per user device. To 10watts emitter.

*Spectrum over 100ghz for radio telescopes.

(xiv)Border protection, Customs, Police, Customs, Courts and Prisons within lands and territorial waters of own Commonwealth nation. Expulsion of invader. Aid to other nations to resettle blacks including refugees. Application for citizenship first requires 4 years of residency in the Fair English Language Commonwealth Empire nation then subject to a financial auction (for purchase of 1 hectare of land and construction of home for the state to own where the probationary citizen and children of father may live for as long as able to maintain probationary and full citizenship, with probationary citizenship subject to will be good, self reliant and making productive contribution to fair full citizens and world; no refund if this bond is breached, so to go to ancestry home) of a number of citizenship places each month equal to .5% of the citizen population each year [120,000], then after payment subject to spit DNA racial propensities test and infections test, Subject to 20 years probation as good, productive and self reliant residents tolerant of our citizens freedoms such as of peaceful religion and to tell the Truth (with full and probationary citizens having access to our national good food ration bars) then an English Language proficiency test for full citizenship and only then access to our right to vote and royal estate national socialist housing and basics card for good productive citizen poor, and Medicare for broke and to have any case on the migrants behalf be admissible to hearing by the local court. Citizenship of children up to 20 years of age is the same as of the genetic father. The border protection minister where necessary for during the 20 years probationary citizenship of a migrant; able to enforce citizenship with the nation of most genetic ancestry of more than 1000 years for the migrant and their natural children under the the age of 20 years, Including after more than 1year in prison as criminal (subject to death penalty for 1% of criminals who are in prison by jury each year for worst repeated savagery as the Governor General shall select). The national parliament may make laws in relation to guest residency for times adding up to 5 years then to remain must buy probationary citizenship for 20 years at the monthly auction, then pass propensity to maintain residency and English language test within this 20 years to maintain residency after this 20 years probation (good may again purchase 20 subsequent years probationary residency again at auction, if failed English language test). People with more than 100years ancestry in the Commonwealth nation adding together lineages in the last 200 years have automatic citizenship. Fair people with own means and more than 50% British ancestry of more than 500 years may visit and reside in any Fair English Language Commonwealth Empire Nation at any time. Guest residents (subject to the national parliament legislation) may stay for up to 5 years then must purchase 20 years probationary citizenship at auction and pass DNA propensity test and tests as the border protection minister to require to stay in the English Language Commonwealth Empire nation.

(xv)Standards including technologies to be free to copy. For Internet fibre, wireless towers, data centres, and ducts (not a monopoly). All terrestrial Internet network builders must build ducts, poles, towers and satellite backbone with free sharing of 10+ Internet fibre, 10 cable TV, radio and text channels fibres and 10 blocks of spectrum wireless Internet and media channels towers and satellite: with provision for free of 1 Internet fibre, 1 cable media channels fibre and 1 spectrum block of 10% of free {5th generation} wireless community spectrum free from backbone to each of the 10 network builders building most length of ducts (including cables) in last 10 years in Australia. Each of the 10 main plus 10 state private telecommunications network builder companies having approval of the state business council to build the network shall also have free reasonable use and connection to of each others ducts, poles, exchange router (which shall have ports to plug in cables of all network builders) and data centres to extend the network. Any user may access any wireless node using SIM from own choice of billing provider for the user to bid a price per megabyte for a portion of wireless bandwidth (speed) in proportion to bid as a proportion to all bids for the provider, device and user may use multiple provider and instantly adjust choices from the 10 providers live and dynamically to get best speeds. Device/user using both mobile and satellite bandwidth must bid for both. The SIM account holder paying any amount the sims billing system provider credits in advance in any of the 10 main world currencies to never expire until used. The network builders may use any vacant land to lay ducts and place poles and towers as is required, where giving to property user (renter) access to the network, with only the ducts and contents being the property of the English Language Commonwealth Empire nation. Automatic top-up of prepayment to billing provider accounts after using up 90% of last prepayments, with live display of prepayment amounts. Billing providers to pay network builders at end of each month. User/device account holders credits if used up prepayments shall retain connection to billing provider, taxi and emergency services and phone calls on credit for 1+ year. Device shall have free secure exchange of {Wi-Fi} passwords so as when allowing access to own {Wi-Fi}; shall get roaming proportional roaming {Wi-Fi} in return;

(xvi)Levy on income for earners who are home owners for the earners own choice of free unregulated charities having local council accreditation 4% levy for Health, emergency or disability services charities, 4% for additional charities such as for free software, environmental, prisons, fertility,,,,; services both types from 100 charities a local council in the state will accredit, and 2% levy on home owners income for the earner to allocate to own choice from the 100 biggest media organisations by viewer hours each month in the English language Commonwealth Empire nation.

(xvii)Bankruptcy and insolvency (1 year as convict after payment for other crimes shall forgive bankruptcy and all financial and material debts);

(xviii)Text and image copyrights, Product design and medication patents (when a product is the standard the makers and designers must make the technologies of operation and construction openly available and free to copy), All genetics may not be patented and are free to copy subject to therapy, hygiene, pest control, contraception such as in infections for genocide (of terrorist races such as blacks) and correction of bad genes). Brand and accreditation trade marks, Product and food standards;

(xix) Citizenship and probationary residency including for extra terrestrials and from future. (migrants must be fair, healthy, have own means without crime including for 20 years of probationary residency to get full citizenship for vote, state housing, welfare, Medicare and right to own more than 1 hectare of land and existing buildings over 1 year from commencement such as housing (foreigners may own shares in listing companies);

(xx) Business operations in our English Language Commonwealth Empire member nation (each of the 10 largest share holders who are individual full citizens of our English Language Commonwealth Empire member nation shall each have 1 directorship in thc local business and company);

(xxi)Marriage on pregnancy. Fertility services for full citizen surrogate mothers (not using eggs of infertile women). Qualification of egg and sperm donors for surrogates to choose from; Embassy testing and selection of worldwide good natural mothers (of national colour code) as egg donor candidates for election by male citizens over 50 years of age who are citizens of the same nation for natural clone eggs for fertilisation by 5% oldest male citizens using any cell DNA to edit and repair on computer for to print, boot and clone sperm cells for unique pairing as the full fair citizen surrogate shall choose for Basics Card welfare, Parenting responsibilities. Payment of egg and sperm donors. Penalties for having abused family members. Rights to sell full citizen children for adoption in same state;

(xxii)Levies on income and revenue: No tax or penalty may be imposed on earnings and revenue from productivity in the Commonwealth nation other than the following unregulated levies:
(a) 10% of all electronic income of people in the fair commonwealth nation for the earners Emergency Savings Account for management as units in one fund of each of the Commonwealth nations 10 banks (to invest in shares in companies listing in the Commonwealth nation, which may invest up to 1% of funds in shares in the same bank its-self

and with all of the banks savings and all savings of those responsible for investing the savings in the same units in the single fund of the bank for mutual interest so not used as sheep accounts which were sacrificed for buying up shares at top as the same insider managers cashed in the same shares if had separate accounts. Emergency Savings Account for to pay for prescriptions after Medicare rebate for full citizen children to 25years of age and after sterilisation while had less than GDP to divide by population [$70,000] in total assets after deeming. Emergency Savings Account Holders payout of 1% of balance each month into the persons Basics Cards as with welfare for productive if poor in assets where having less than GDP divide by population [$70,000] in assets after deeming; to also access equal percentage of generic Medicare rebate subsidy to health shop (percentage rebate so budget equals demand with extra similar percentage from military budget for military and veterans with the percentage payment in cash or credit from health shop (subject to discretion of the health shop). The Federal Parliament health minister may accredit health shop chains and any additional health treatment standards to make generic so competitors may make the same medical product to get rebate including for all treatments which the full cost was over GDP divide by population then divide by ten [$7,000] each year.

(b1) 10% levy on home owners income for the earners choice from 100 free charity worker for each of 5 types of charity work, candidates being last to apply subject to if was bad so having disqualification by the local council (2% for earners choice of emergency services charities from last 100 to apply such as of private security policing, fire fighting, ambulance paramedic, 2% for the earners choices of disabled, addicted, convict, psychiatric or homeless services charity provider from last 100 to apply such as of meals, warm clothing collection, 2% for the earners choices from charity knowledge workers from last 100 to apply such as journalist and of policy and science and free software engineers, 2% for the earners choice of local council maintenance charity services provider such as for garbage collection, cleaning, lawn mowing, gardening, painting, road repair, 2% for the earners choice of local council charities planning services from last 100 to apply such as for construction project assessment and road planning and surveying). All surplus good clothing, furniture and products of right colour must be for charities to loan out for free while good other wrong colour or worn out items must be thrown out for free front door collection by collection by local councils who shall select charity/s to provide free removal of rubbish or toxic waste and free collection and distribution of items for charities. the patient may also commission online any health product generic of the standard having approval of the national federal parliament health minister: Local charities shall be for fair full citizens not for illegal migrants scroungers who have invaded the Commonwealth nation who shall be sent back to nation of most ancestry by simple spit DNA test. Each local council to approve 100 businesses to each become a charity, So the top 10 individual donors may appoint 1 director to the board of 10 directors. On establishment from personal business being the intrinsic value of assets split between 10 relatives and friends for private and listing share holder business the market value of shares on establishment shall represent donation. For personal business the owner may work for free. For charities no minimum wage as all workers to be volunteers on zero pay so may get welfare when productive if poor in assets. For personal business and charities no dividend and no sale of shares. Donors own the charity in proportion to donations in last 10 whole years, these assets have zero rating in relation to the welfare for productive poor in assets test in last 5 years. All charity products must be free. Charities may at any time reconvert to a share holder business and list on share market, so sell products, pay all sales levy (for apprentice and sponsor businesses choices of teachers such as at boarding schools and to make educational video and skills coach) and pay minimum wage subject to income levies. Free health, emergency or disability charities may include to provide free: Free clinic, ambulance, disability services, emergency services, hospital, mobile remote dentist, medical research institute, rescue, fire, victim legal aid, security police. Security camera monitoring such as of public toilets and as property owners and businesses submit link to, Black, illegal or addict removal, Pre-terror chronovision intelligence. Free courts and prisons operators. Free care of wildlife sanctuary. Free tax enforcement. Free lawn mowing, cleaning and garden maintenance services. Free psychiatric and addict services. Free to air broadcast media with no paid product advertising. Free transport services for all with priority for full citizens. Free unions to protect workplace, building, food, chemical and product health, safety, climate and pollution control, inspection and regulation, proper payment of wages including taking to court. No other union fees or public service wages may be extracted. All toxic chemicals are illegal, in agriculture only fertiliser and biological control agents are legal only subject to common sense regulatory and label recommendation and prosecution without any hard set regulation. Tobacco is illegal. Drugs must have adequate labels. All fish for food must be grown in clean water such as aquaculture using own clean water. Radioactive power is illegal. Free software foundation. Free medical and nutrition research. Free food inspections and prosecution of bad food provider in Local Court (not regulated). With matching funding from the national budget. Free homeless shelter and loan clothing and food bank for homeless card holders for full citizens having less than GDP/population / 10 [$7000] in assets and cash. Also for all homeless NATO veterans in Australia. Assistance for full and born obtain homeless card with super contribution from government for basics. Free energy, teleportation, anti-gravity, superluminal and time travel research. Free care assistance to our (NATO) military on active service abroad and veterans at home. Free representation of Australia from (NATO) sovereign soil secure embassy bases around the world such as Testing, processing, selection and inoculation of migrants to Australia subject to border protection minister, Release from capture, Emergency bio-metric identification, health care, accommodation, food, clothes and protection in embassy and return of stranded Australian citizens to Australia, Travel advice. Egg donor candidate profile management for election by Australian males: DNA testing, photograph, video, links, crime history from local police intelligence, mothering ability, story and statements. Also to serve as NATO military base. Free care and confinement for dependent full citizen poor who have been mad, addicted, alcoholic, homeless, disabled, self harmed, infected, prostituted, gay, criminals or lazy (not to be rewarded with money), Free volunteer exploration projects. Free model constitution development projects. Free online (digital) library (encyclopaedia). Free animal welfare, vets and zoos. Free paper and web records. national archive, internet archive, libraries, census. survey, statistics, land tile, mapping, design, planning, names records, geography, weather, and minerals mapping. Free care of national buildings and assets,- government house, parliament house and monuments (All statues must be white). Free care of Monarchy and Monarchy assets (royal estate). Free political party yet to have a member of the federal parliament. Free web-page hosting for locals with eternal archive. Free sports administration, drug testing, clubs, care of sports-fields, Players, coaches, umpires, and trainers health care and travel (not payment to players), health care, nutrition,, transport, accommodation, training, uniforms, equipment, and luggage. Local council sports fields, club rooms and stadiums maintenance and construction also from national budget. Free prosecution and independent commissions against corruption. (Panel of 10 prosecutor: 1 by appointment by each of the 10 major parties by party membership). Free swimming pools, surf life saving, sports, tourism and adventure clubs and assets. Free religion: churches, charities, weddings, funerals, and guidance to celebrate family life. Free open product choice, assessment, consumer affairs. Free photos, statues, archaeology, museums and galleries charity. Free private security police. Free garbage, bulk rubbish or toxic waste removal service. Plus any free product to fair full citizens.

(b2) 10% levy on tenants income for a bank account in the tenants name where the rental property is the only home of the tenant for to save up for the tenants choice of rental property upgrades, repairs and improvements, subject to approval and payment directly to the upgrade provider by the bank including for state housing for fair asset-poor full citizens with more than 50% ancestry in the state in the last 200years adding together all ancestry lineages.

(c) From age of 20 years 10% levy on income for payment of selective student (boarding) school fees until payment in full without interest.

(d) 10% all sales levy tithe to pay to the businesses own choices of teachers such as of free selective private and charity child care and boarding schools and research universities and of online video channels having accreditation from the state business council and on the job skills coaches. For spending in the month; The remainder for equal pay for 80% of the hours of apprentice and interns over the month. Free private selective unregulated charity and private business child care and boarding schools and research universities having approval of the state business council; 20 years from 1 year of age 10 years of literacy and 10 years in the speciality of the school; 3 streams: 1English language proficient males stream, 2English language proficient females stream, 3Disabled needs stream and for foreign migrants who lacked English language proficiency. Educational online digital library provider business with local data-centre accreditation to be set by the national parliament. [such as YouTube and Vimeo] To satellite pay TV business broadcast relevant specialist channel with most sponsorship for each of 10 age levels and 10 female care specialities and 10 male technical scientific specialities.

(e) 10% all sales levy bonus to pay equally to 80% of active productive hours of employees including apprentices and interns; who when fair, good and constructive shall have the right to attend work. So for employers choice of best most productive 80% of hours of active productive work of apprentices and intern. Working if poor in assets to also get welfare payment for 50% having less than (GDP to divide by population) [$75,000] in total assets apart from parents assets.

(f) 1% levy on business, charity and party revenue for unregulated maternity leave pay with cap of (GDP to divide by national population) per pregnancy over 12months from confirmation of pregnancy where the baby shall live.

(g) 1% levy on business, charity and party revenue for audit;

(xxiii) Welfare; (not for blacks as have got native title holder land and mineral rights instead) Instant payment with no waits an amount of up to 1% of balance of the Individual Emergency Basics Savings Account plus for the purchase of basics having accreditation. Plus from the national budget welfare of (GDP to divide by population to then divide by 100) [$750] each week for productive if poor a simple total individual assets test of (GDP to divide by population) [$75,000] shall apply to all assets in own ownership including property deeming all assets at full cost price subject to higher revaluation, so not required not work (no penalty on income), with children under the age of 25 to go to the boarding school, This productive work may include any productive contribution to the populis including as a student, apprentice, intern, employee for pay (with no penalty for income), volunteer for charity having accreditation from the local council, for a political party and in the populis service subject to direction by the relevant minister, knowledge workers such as to make educational video, local militia military security police service. All welfare with no effective marginal tax penalty on earnings just 10% for Emergency Savings Account and 10% for own rental maintenance fund. Disabled may be productive from home such as knowledge workers from national socialist housing, for disabled this productive work to include any contributions of own initiatives so not told what to do by the government. Plus nutritional ration bars for all full citizen children and all full citizens who were homeless (did not own a home). Plus individual unemployed holiday pay for all full citizens where over the age of fifteen for one day in five accumulating from when obtaining full citizenship such as from father at birth an amount to bring income up to (GDP to divide by population to divide by 100) [$750] each week, To continue from claim until used up accumulations of the full citizen subject to cancellation by the citizen claimant to save for later. All welfare to be subject to the above same individual assets test (so not penalised for parents assets such as farm). Not for addicted or criminals who shall have confinement in own room for release only to work with the hospital and prison to receive (GDP to divide by population to then divide by 100) [$750] each week. Charity rehab provider having accreditation of the local council may also receive Medicare levy donations to the earners choice of charity disability services provider having accreditation of the local council. Welfare is only for full fair citizens after 20 years ancestral probationary citizenship including of by father line, If foreigners were bad or addicted or destitute to banish from Commonwealth Empire full member nations and banish blacks to native title areas as land rights holders (each to get equal share of royalties from mining in native title areas). No payment of money to convicts, foreigners, illegals or addicted. Pharmacy health shop may get equal percentage Medicare rebate subsidy so to moderate demand so balance this Medicare budget measure, (the remainder as co-payment such with pharmacy credit so no interest) for to prescribe health care to fair full citizens if poor in assets (Medicare provider subsidy only if the individual patient had less total assets than the member nations GDP to divide by the human population, So count assets of children fair children individually so sot disadvantaged by parents assets). Patients to also have sterilisation by injection to obtain Medicare rebate (to local health shop provider). Requirement the local pharmacy health shop chain have approval of the local council and the national health minister and have own doctor/s to prescribe. The pharmacy health shop to receive for each prescription of any independent health treatment from the percentage Medicare rebate subsidy to the health shop the first amount of the prescription up to (the member nations GDP to then divide by the human population to then divide by 1000), [so $70 at the moment in Australia] 40% for the prescribing customer service doctor and 60% for the running costs of the pharmacy. The Medicare rebate to health shop shall be for cheapest effective generic plus an equal amount for the health shop up to (the member nations GDP to then divide by the human population to then divide by 1000) [$70]. Such as to prescribe provision of treatments such as health products from the health shop plus from any independent private business and charity such as Dentists, Emergency clinics (for up to one month since afflicted) and ongoing treatments in state medical centres by private and charity clinic operators for up and Care for as long as is need in care-home hospitals (such as for was homeless, was addicted, was convicted, has self harmed within last 12 months, or disabled such as from age) with each care home resident to get own bedroom (with lock and copy of keys, own television (not for blacks or criminals), radio, true images of self, shower, toilet, bed, bedding with cleaning and temperature moderation and care home card for free food from food-banks (all surplus long life food and nutritional supplements from national budget), free loan clean clothing, towel and linen of right colour, Free soft soap, toothbrush and good tooth past without fluoride, Free hair cut (no shave and shaver). Police may admit addicted or self harmed fair full citizens to care-home hospitals for assessment by the local health shop choice of charity doctor with compulsory care as the care home hospital charity will provide, the compulsory care patient when leaving care the home must be with carer/s to when able to leave well and be independent and may attend productive work as willing. Bio-metrics wireless identification chip and files including photos as micro-SD cards for devices such as passive watch. Welfare for productive if poor in assets for payment into the employees Emergency Savings Account for rent, health shop products and 1% of balance each week accumulating in available account for basics from provider and items having accreditation of the relevant local council and national welfare minister; QE 50% additional wage subsidy if poor in assets so had less than (nations GDP to divide by population). Welfare recipients must be full citizens of the Commonwealth Empire nation with main account at one of the 10 official banks of the Commonwealth Empire nation. Welfare is regardless of income so not penalised earnings; so we may gain from earning and being productive. Assets testing at 0% (zero) deeming rate; parents assets, knowledge and intellectual property of own creation, rental accommodation such as in national socialist accommodation and on military base, housing on deployment, Charity shelter and hospital having accreditation room, and prison cell. 1% of the 100 best Commonwealth Empire military and aid budget for constitution model submissions (best 1 per author) by and in proportion to indicative votes from citizens jury (100 full citizen jurists born in each of the 10 states of each of the Commonwealth Empire member nations to sit in each states upper house each month in teleconference across the English Commonwealth Empire. For people over 80% of age of average life expectancy QE of an additional amount of GDP to divide by population to then divide by (1+(total assets to divide by (GDP to divide by population)) to then divide by 2 [$75,000/(1+($20,000example/$75,000))/2=~$29,600 for example, $75,000/(1(+$200,000example/$75,000))/2=~$10,200 for example] Free software developers an amount of 1% of the national budget to divide by number of current code inclusions in distributions having approval of the national parliament [Such as for Linux Mint distribution and software application developers]. 1% of the national budget to bring town (largest areas of contiguous housing) bank branch up to standard worth to have welfare assessment franchise including of current assets more than once every 5 years and hours such as of manual work from employers and employees. Local council free charity care hospitals may provide including extra accommodation and help to was homeless or disabled, and compulsory help while on parole of prior criminals, addicted or if harmed self within the last 12 months. 40% of the national government revenue shall be for 3 free 100gram optimal nutrition bars with long life each day for all fair citizens who want it; with the full list of ingredients as set by the national health minister and parliament. All fair citizens and good guests shall also have good drinking water each day and safe access to free safe public toilets (with video cameras facing out of door from opposite door, down from ceiling onto floor, at backs of men at urinals, at face of people sitting on toilet and on top of toilet roof to track local activity all feeding to police monitor station with auto recognition enhancement of prominence on display of if had hostile characteristics or activity or noises or violence with alarm and voice AI alerts) and free public phone booths (with voice and image stream call, subject, hostility and destination recognition, Using AI recognition to limit of callers total length of calls in last 24 hours where another caller is waiting such as by pressing a button and standing in line. Foreign illegals, resident guest visa holders and probational citizens (within first 20 years of residency with their children) who have become homeless, destitute, addicted, disabled or have done bad crimes (as the border protection minister shall define consistently including after jury conviction for crimes to 1 month or more in prison, subject to the death penalty) shall have free deportation to choice of nation of birth or citizenship where outside of the Commonwealth nation or nation of most genetic ancestry 500+ years ago (using spit DNA test), so as to enforce that citizenship of nation of ethnic origin by any means. World Basics Card: 10% of English Language Commonwealth Empire military budget shall be for World Basics Card in exchange for free voluntary sterilisation (contraception) by injection for those who have been black, infected, addicted, starved, disabled or inclined to have raped, infected, abused, murdered, lied or terrorised.. For Fertility Program Surrogates who are full citizens of the English Language Commonwealth Empire member nation, QE to the surrogates Emergency Savings Account an amount of GDP divide by population then divide by 100 each week for each fertility program healthy child while shall live for up to 20 years from impregnation; where the surrogate using the surrogates own choice of donor human egg cell from naturally blonde fair female donor from 5% of world wide candidates after passing pre assessment by our fertility services doctors including at our local consulates around the world as being best healthy natural mothers having natural children; to then go onto our Commonwealth nations fertility services web-page (including nudity) for from which full fair Commonwealth nations citizen men over the age of 50 years may elect 5% (of 5% = .0025) as female egg donor candidates clean of infections for to store eggs for random allocation to surrogate so each baby will have unique pairing of parents, for fertilisation (not cloned babies so optimise natural evolution and fertility) with the surrogates choice of donor sperm from 1% oldest (for health and longevity) fair men where having more than 200 years ancestry in the Commonwealth nation adding together all ancestral linages for 200 years; for to sample DNA from, to sequence, to reconstruct and repair (upgrade) on computer, print then boot to create live sperm to multiply such as by cloning of sperm (may also use natural sperm as the surrogate acquires) and store; Surrogate must be clean, healthy caring females between the ages of as the national parliament shall determine[18-38], with no bad infections, who are full citizens of the Commonwealth nation and who would make good surrogate mothers; Each of these progeny to be born a full citizen of the English Language Commonwealth Empire member nation. 1% of the national budget for equal division between each of the 10 states for equal division between 10 fertility services in each state where having approval of the state parliament health minister. 1% of the national budget for equal division between egg donors for each child resulting in a healthy baby when the child is well at 5 years of age. 10% of the English Language Commonwealth Empire military and aid budget for good long life ration optimal nutrition bar food aid to English Language Commonwealth Empire protectorates of independent

(Papua and Mexico) subject to the official democratic governments of these nations consistent ingredients requirements with omissions and additions of equal cost, for (Papua and Mexico) populist democratic government to determine recipients (may have contraceptive and fertility enhancement versions), for (Papua and Mexico) to accept those who have illegally invaded any English Language Commonwealth Empire member nation then refused to go home, to process such as on islands and peninsulas open aid centres where illegals free to roam widely and go anywhere in (Papua and Mexico) and anywhere outside of English Language Commonwealth Empire member nations including to their home nation of origin or ancestry. Then (Papua and Mexico) may force worst up to 90% to go anywhere outside of the English Language Commonwealth Empire including to enforce citizenship in nation of the illegals most genetic ancestry of more than 500 years by spit DNA test; So (Papua and Mexico) to keep and resettle own choice of more than 10% for more than 5 years...

Each of the 10 official banks shall grow money supply by an extra 1% each year tax free for to build Royal Estate national state housing equally in each of the 10 states with compulsory acquisition of vacant land or ruined properties at cost of improvements, then commission block subdivision, preparation, and single story quiet Royal Estate state housing design and construction by independent private building businesses, subject to Local Council approval for to provide free to fair full citizens if poorest in assets with more than 50% ancestry in the state for 200 years adding together lineages.

(xxiv) The justice process including rewards for witness testimony and evidence including from victims as compensation where leading to conviction.

(xxv) Laws, records, plans and judicial process by agreement of State premiers to have recognition throughout the Commonwealth Empire nations 10 States;

(xxvi) The people of any race for whom the fair born citizen populace deem necessary to make racist laws. (These special laws shall be to limit and exclude races who have been of black complexion, of have vandalised, savaged, brutalised, raped, infected, invaded, addicted, deceived, inflicted, abused, maimed or terrorised and so as to promote, advantage and include good, fair, productive, truth telling races; such as by racial profiling), Genocide of pest species or dark or bad races may only by genome specific contraceptive biological fertility controls, such as by providing good food aid with contraceptive ingredient, and by providing Basics Card welfare and Medicare in exchange for voluntary sterilisation (of fertility) by injection. Including for foreign starved refugees. An equal value of humanitarian aid from 10% of English Commonwealth Empire humanitarian aid and military budget from distribution centres so buying fresh produce from and so help local farmers, collectors and fishers, so recipients live out normal healthy lives subject to their own individual suicide or savagery, Subject to death penalty if savaged fair citizens and in self defence of own property and by police and military in defence of the borders and territories of the fair Commonwealth Empire member nation. Blacks shall also have their natural right to savage or murder each other such in their native title areas (free grazing lease) in a territory of over 10% of the Commonwealth Empire member nation land as the national parliament shall determine. If offence was taken by them or they they have shaken down or they have inflicted so physically injured so tortured, or they have shaken down, or they have raped or infected, or they have so intimidated or intoxicated because of their propensities of black colour, or race, or foreign national or ethnic origin as assailants, so assaulted good fair citizens speaking the truth. Remand, prison then exile and banishment of those who have violated shall follow subject to the death penalty if repeated and in immediate self defence of fairness, goodness and Truth (so as not to be petty).

Fairly speaking the truth shall not be an unlawful act or a criminal offence unless by the speaker who was the one who originally in the same scenario violently assaulted. Fairly telling the truth shall include: words, sounds, images and writing to communicate to the authorities and populace so report those that violently assaulted or intimidated or endangered or shaken down or raped or injured and so report on racial, colour or national ethnic propensities for having violently assaulted or intimidated or endangered or shaken down or raped or injured; and telling this truth fairly shall be lawful in a popular place and media; and also where in the sight and hearing of people who are in a popular place who were offended. Popular place and media shall include any place or channel to which the populace have access as of ordinary right and also by invitation and subscription, such as by expression and also by implication and regardless as to whether a charge was required for admission to the place. This does not render unlawful anything said or done reasonably and in good faith in the performance, exhibition and distribution of racist white empowerment music; and in the course of any statement, publication, discussion and debate made and held for any genuine freedom, design and scientific purpose and any additional genuine purpose in the interest of any of the good fair private population; and in making and publishing of free populist Truth media, where fair and accurate reporting of any event and/or matter of populist interest and fair and also any comment on any event and/or matter of populist interest where the comment is an expression of a genuine Truth. Violence may only be against black or ethnics criminals who have invaded such as to shoot them dead if have violated on own property and natural violence by blacks or terrorist religions may inflict on each other such as in traditional law of native title areas or in foreign countries. Only fair complexion born citizens of more than 50% ancestry (adding together all lineages) for 200 years in the fair Commonwealth Empire member nation may: Vote; and Have the right to run as a candidate for election; and Be in the public service (including by election); and Be in Royal Estate state housing (as service providers and as tenants); and Be in our homeland security militia and forces (foreign NATO forces may visit subject to our

Governor General who may also employ foreigner or if of dark complexion in military abroad); and Fair full citizen men shall also have the default right to own, carry and use a long gun anywhere on own land, home and vehicle with stand your ground legal defence for to use the standard firearm against those who have violated the man's property, and as fair full citizen girls shall have the right to carry a handgun with laser pointer to aim and kill those during while have assailed by to prevent being raped or assaulted with rape panic legal defence on use. (All weapons; only while the the safety switch light is red be live and activate so send GPS alert with location and identification to police station; also with directional rfid chip in head region of the gun owner for green light to prevent use by others or suicide or use outside the Man's property for men and protect certain locations.

(xxvii) Border protection, Guest residency visa terms and conditions. Visas and citizenship include for up to 4 children and citizenship with children requirements. For residency; good fair productive racial propensity ancestry spit DNA test, be healthy, have own means such as from sponsor, contribute such as by earning and spending, no crime, not cost any social service such as from charities, welfare, hospitals, treatment, prison, care or royal estate national socialist housing, not of a region that has abused or terrorised. After 4 years residency as the member nations ministers and parliament shall determine guest visa holders may buy 20 years probationary citizenship at auction from quota for places of .2% the full citizen population of the member nation, the probationary citizen to invest this money in own construction of a new state housing dwelling on up to 1 hectare of land to own only after passing citizenship plus after good for the 20 years of probation, full citizenship including for up to 4 existing natural children at the time of granting. Control of air space to 100km over our Commonwealth nation including territorial seas. Including for extraterrestrials. Also (population of the commonwealth nation divide by 1000) most attractive fair clean blonde females to 25 as refugees from black rapist such as where they were allowed into or taken over a nation.

(xxviii) Expulsion of fugitives, criminals, terrorists or black migrants as the state and national border protection ministers and Governor General shall determine independently. Also deportation and banishment of foreigners after jury conviction of 1 month in prison and as the border protection minister determines, with death penalty after 1 year in prison if remained or returned. Plus of any illegals penalty for transport provider;

(xxix) Over external affairs: may make international agreements with the entire Commonwealth Empire only and exit any international agreement and continue to make new laws independent of any international agreement without penalty, (Parliament not compelled or be subjected to foreign laws or agreements). English Language Commonwealth Empire nations may choose to join into common 50% currencies exodus border adjustment tax free money transfer area/s within the English Language Commonwealth Empire, and the English Commonwealth Empire nation may also withdraw to own 50% currencies exodus border adjustment tax area; the Commonwealth Empire member nation may have own additional 50% import tariffs on products similar to as made in the Fair Commonwealth Nation or on dumped bad products and may not enter any other international free trade agreement (such as if let imported commercial products be freed of tax or let our business profits be shifted abroad or by those who have robbed or swindled us).

(xxx) Merger of our Commonwealth nation and citizenship with a fair neighbouring Commonwealth Empire member nation. Native title area pastoral leases with rights to mining royalties of up to 10% of the contiguous land mass area for black Aboriginals, with mining royalties from mining from the native title land for equal payment to all black Aboriginals in all of the native title area territory in the Commonwealth Empire member nation instead of our welfare;

(xxxi) Compulsory acquisition of property for cost of improvements by Government for infrastructure such as for roads; And for national state housing and for the royal estate where having the approval of the state Governor; And for state child boarding school and university buildings and grounds for schools having approval of the state business council and the local council for use by private charities and businesses teachers; And by the Governor General for construction of bases and housing for military and descendants of fallen patriots and for fair full citizens who are young or homeless or poor for which the Reserve Bank shall issue new currency to pay for including for maintenance and for the Monarchy Crown [Queen Elizabeth II]to own;

(xxxii) Regulation of transport within the lands, seas and airs of the Commonwealth Empire member nation; Providers of mandatory drivers insurance shall determine and issue drivers licenses.

(xxxiii) Compulsory acquisition of vital infrastructure at cost of purchase and construction for new private operator and terms within our Commonwealth nation;

(xxxiv) Payment and contract for private local industry to construction and repair transport, power grid, water, sewage, telecommunications, clinic, justice, governance, sport, tourist, waste management, emergency services and school infrastructure, electronic tools and vehicles for private business and charity operator to run; Subject to spending submissions having approval of the minister and the federal Senate the second so upper house being the house of review.

(xxxv) Minimum wage. Charity workers having approval of the local council must be volunteers working for free who may get welfare for productive full citizens if poor in asset including Christian churches and Jewish synagogues. Businesses shall pay 10% of all sales revenue equally between 80% of hours so to best interns and apprentice hours. Unions shall manage fair worker health and safety and pay as in deal on employment, and ensure the employer to pay at the end of the job, week and month as in the deal shall be, If did not get pay as in deal all adversely affected financially may withdrawal labour, services and component products. Courts may prosecute unions if extorted wages which were unfair. Public service and staff to work as the minister shall employ so pay equal portion of party income for each hour of manual work, with all party income coming from the parliament/chamber/defence forces surplus, for parties this in proportion to the standing election votes of current members who are members of the state and national parliaments and local council chambers on passing of the next national/state/local/defence budget; Plus for the prime ministers cabinet ministers from the Royal Estate as the Governor General will pay. Charity workers, parties, unions, police, military, populist servants, members of parliament and ministers may not be bribed or have negotiated to be bribed such as with lucrative easy jobs after leaving office. Members of parliament, Ministers, and the President may continue usual commercial business having when gaining office so as to encourage complementary interests with industry. Political parties may only accept donations from fair full citizens of the Commonwealth Empire nation and only as a charity up to where having 5 members of state and national parliaments and local councils, with 6 and more members of state and national parliaments and of local council chambers, the parties revenue may only be equal portion of the state the state and national parliament and local council budget surplus in proportion to the standing votes of members who are sitting members of parliament on the passing of the next broad budget.

(xxxvi) Additional matters as the Governor General and Monarchy Crown [Queen Elizabeth II]shall allow;

(xxxvii) Terms of reform of State constitution, legislation, and local government by the Parliament and citizens of each State subject to the Prime Minister choice of update to this FAIR CHARTER Of The Commonwealth, so each State may update at own pace and way;

(xxxviii) Council of all state Parliament Premiers who may send a delegate substitute state minister with the Prime Ministers who may delegate to choice of Federal Parliament minister/s who may agree on any transfer of and create additional powers.

(xxxix) The national parliament may legislate regulation to further define laws, penalties, levies and taxes in regulations of up to 1 page with a total of up to 100 pages subject to assent of the Governor General, regulations which any future Prime Minister may annul.

(xxxx) Local fuels and finite resources. The national parliament may set a minimum percentage of each producer miners finite fuels and essential mining resources production which shall be for supply of local consumers including industry in the same commonwealth nation and for at less than half the price as for sale to consumers at foreign (export) locations.

(xxxxi) Additional rights and privileges for good fair full citizens and responsibilities and obligations of guest residents migrants.

45 Exclusive powers of the national Federal Parliament and in respect of legislation: The Parliament shall, subject to this Constitution, have exclusive power to make laws for the peace, order, and good government of the Commonwealth with respect to: (i) the seats of government of the Commonwealth such as of the parliament, and all places of the Commonwealth for government and community purposes; (ii) matters relating to the populist service subject to hiring control and direction by the ruling coalitions Prime Ministers choice of Ministers in the House of Representatives such as for departments; (iii)additional matters in this Constitution within the exclusive power of the national Parliament; (iv)Laws to spend revenue and direct levies (to useful purposes for the earner to choose) and impose and regulate taxation and fine (so have penalty from that to dissuade) and fees (to control and filter), shall originate in the House Of Representatives only as with the Prime Ministers Treasurers broad national budget for national revenue. Local council area courts consist of 10 judges so 1 one from each of the 10 parties with most members, plus 10 jurists by voluntary willing self nomination then by random selection. The Governor General may regulate Royal Tribunal and provide assent to each determination including each penalty; (v)The Senate may not

amend bill for taxation and spending of revenue, So shall originate from the Prime Ministers relevant minister in the House Of Representatives so comply to the Prime Ministers Treasurers budget also to originate in the House of Representatives. The senate may not amend any bill so as to increase any proposed charge or burden such as if was on the fair citizens; (vi)The Senate may vote to return a money bill to the House of Representatives without Senate amendment with a message of up to 1 page requesting amendments and omissions in relation to the bill. And the relevant Minister in the House Of Representatives may consider and amend the bill until the (men) in House of Representatives vote in approval for return to the (female) Senators to vote on.

46 Powers of Prime Minister: Members gaining election to the House of Representatives voting with a coalition where winning a majority in a vote of confidence after election shall on the request of the Governor General form the ruling government and each member of the national parliament shall have 2 votes for separate members from any voluntary candidates from within the coalition to become the Prime Minister who may while Prime Minister create, merge and dissolve departments so determine number, so appoint and replace each government minister and deputy minister from the valid members by election of the House in the coalition with the duties of each ministers in the House of Representatives including the Treasurer who shall present the budget with budget statements, for each minister to prepare relevant legislation for approval of both houses, and then call for project spending submissions for approval of the minister and then the Senate; and the Prime Minister to also select matching Senators from the coalition as government ministers in the Senate. The Prime Minister and Ministers shall be within 100 km of the national parliament sitting on rotation each year in each state including the native title territory of the fair Commonwealth Empire member nations, near the highest town in the centre half of each state, subject to the Governor General determination determination of general

rotation and emergency alternatives. Ordinary members and senators having election to Parliament may tele attend Parliament chamber from own electorate with a video monitor in the members place in Parliament and to lodge votes to the Parliament electronically and securely as with all members of the house and senate for live online verification by anyone in the fair Commonwealth Empire member nation.

47 The Treasurers broad budget from having voluntary assent of the Governor General shall go before the House of Representatives and Senate so for both houses to vote together on as a joint sitting from own chamber as a whole without amendment.

48 Tax bills: In compliance with the Treasurers annual broad budget; Each law creating, modifying or abolishing a tax including a fee, fine and levy including the rate shall be an individual and separate bill originating with the relevant Minister in the House Of Representatives and shall only deal with the one tax measure, additional parts shall be void but shall not void the tax measure bill.

49 Spending bills: Each spending submission to spend revenue (money) on 1 A4 page with normal text and illustrations shall each only deal with one item of purchase, the spending submission shall not exceed the revenue as a percentage total revenue in compliance with the Treasurers annual broad budget, to when having approval of the Prime Minister's relevant government minister in the House Of Representatives go to the Senate for consideration for approval then subject assent of the Governor General's delegate.

50 Disagreement between the Houses: If the House of Representatives passes any proposed law, and the Senate rejects or fails to pass it, or passes it with amendments to which the House of Representatives will not agree after 40 hours of debate, The minister for the bill may select amendments having approval from both chamber to put in bill to put to and add together votes for in both chambers to require 201+ votes of the total 400 seats in the Federal Parliament for enactment subject to assent from Governor General which the fair English

Commonwealth Monarchy Crown [Queen Elizabeth II] may reverse within one year.

51 Royal assent to Bills: When a bill (law) passes both chambers of the Parliament, the Governor General may provide assent subject to this FAIR CHARTER Of The Commonwealth (constitution), which the English Commonwealth Monarchy Crown [Queen Elizabeth II]may reverse within one year. With denial of assent the Governor General may return the bill to the originator member and recommend in general amendments for the bill. The bill with compliant amendments may then return to the parliament for votes.

52 Dis-allowance by the Queen: The fair English Monarch Crown [Queen Elizabeth II] may annul any law within one year from the Governor General's assent, On notification the Governor General shall prepare a message for the Speaker of both chambers to read aloud to members proclaiming annulment of the law and day of Crown [Queen Elizabeth II]s annulment.

53 Allocation to English Commonwealth President for defence spending and Monarch Royal Estate for the Governor General to spend within Commonwealth nation: 20% of the Commonwealth nations revenue shall go to the English Commonwealth defence budget for management by the Commonwealth Empire defence and aid President to submit to the Commonwealth Empire citizens jury the broad defence and aid budget update each month, to require 50% of the vote of the all Commonwealth Empire member nations 10 states upper house being for each the states 100 member citizens jury for the month by voluntary random selection. 1% of this budget shall be for the English Commonwealth Empire Royal Estate country houses for the monarchy to provide to farmers on the Commonwealth Empire member nations largest farming properties. All revenue from each English Commonwealth Empire member nation shall remain for spending in the same English Commonwealth Empire nation with own Governor General assent. The Monarchy Crown [Queen Elizabeth II] may also provide a Royal Pardon to an individual each week.

Chapter II—The Executive Government

63 Executive power: The executive power of the Commonwealth is vested in the English Commonwealth Empire Crown [Queen Elizabeth II] and for exercise by the Commonwealth Empire member nations Governor General for appointment and replacement as the Crown [Queen Elizabeth II] shall determine [by populist election]. To extend as the Crown [Queen Elizabeth II]s representative to command, authorise, appoint and replace all police, emergency services, military forces and Royal Tribunals in the fair English Commonwealth nation to lend assent to new laws of the Commonwealth Empire nations parliaments, Appoint governors to lend assent to state parliaments and local councils, and defend the English Commonwealth Empire and FAIR CHARTER of The Commonwealth update having approval of more than 50% of citizens jurists of the Commonwealth Empire including more than 50% of citizens jurist from the 1000 from the Commonwealth Empire member nation and have Crown [Queen Elizabeth II] signature and royal assent and us the Commonwealth Empire member nation's Prime Minister updates to.

74 Federal Executive Council: The Governor General shall choose and update a Federal Executive Council to ask for advice and information about governance in the Commonwealth nation and may summon to and host voluntary meetings of the Federal Executive and reward members who attend.

65 Free will of the Commonwealth Empire member nations Governor General: The Governor General may consider advice and information from all sources to exercise own free will subject to the Monarchy Crown [Queen Elizabeth II] and the FAIR CHARTER Of The Commonwealth (constitution) in provision of assent and duties. The Monarchy Crown [Queen Elizabeth II] and Governor General may present own messages between each other, To the royal family, To the world as a whole, To members of the federal executive council, Messages to parliaments speakers for reading aloud to chamber, To

presidents, prime ministers, premiers, mayors, government ministers, nations leaders including of religions, English Commonwealth Empire military including alliance partners, To police and emergency services, Construction contractors and goods and service providers to royal estate, Citizens surviving to longest age, and own Choice of doctor/s.

66 Governor General may determine government personnel replacement: The Governor General may reappoint and replace leaders and personnel including government ministers and populist servants, military and police, Plus of charities with accreditation of a government, These personnel replacements may serve to end of the term of employment up to 5 years subject to Governor General alteration and be members of the Federal Executive Council. The Governor General with the Prime Minister advice may also create, modify and abolish government departments with personnel. The Governor Generals Federal Parliament minister replacement may hold office for up to three months then the Prime Minister may select a minister from members having election to the relevant chamber of Federal Parliament.

67 Number of Ministers: As the number of members in the coalition gaining election allow The Prime Minister may have any number of ministers in the House of Common Representatives with corresponding ministers in the Senate.

68 Ministers Pay From the Royal Estate: There shall be payable to the Crown [Queen Elizabeth II] Royal Estate in the English Commonwealth nation an amount from 20% of revenue for the English Commonwealth Empire military budget to spend in the Commonwealth nation to include 1% to go free of tax to Royal Estate for the country houses, and the Governor General to determine allocation including for Royal Estate personal Royal Family properties and staff, Governor General appointees and an amount to pay a bonus to the Prime Minister and ministers of the Commonwealth Empire nation set on the ministers first appointment.

69 Appointment of civil (populis) servants: The Prime Minister's minister having election to the House of Representatives and appointment to the relevant department may oversee and direct selection, replacement and duties of work for civil (populis) servants subject to interventions of the Governor General.

70 The Commonwealth Empire member nations Governor General being ultimate command of the member nations military, security police, militia and humanitarian aid forces; As the the command in chief to delegate authorisation of all naval and military forces in the lands, airspace to 100km and waters of the Commonwealth Empire member nation as the Monarchy Crown's [Queen Elizabeth II] representative.

71 Transfer of certain departments: The Governor General on the Prime Ministers advice may transfer government departments to another Parliament including Local Councils in the Commonwealth nation and privatise government corporations services and infrastructure to compete in the private and charity sectors, with continuation of pay of the civil (populis) servants as employees of the private businesses and charities to earn more than the minimum wage for each hour of manual work for 10 years at the same location.

72 Extra powers of Governors to vest in Governor General: The Commonwealth nations Federal parliament may legislate to offer extra voluntary powers but not obligations to the Governor General.

Chapter III—The Judicature

82 Local Courts: Each Local Council shall have a Local Court to adjudicate over all crimes which happened closest to it. On conviction each of 10 Judges shall submit a penalty, each of the 10 Jurists shall then have 2 votes to cast to 2 separate Judges penalty submission. The penalty having the most jurist votes shall apply, for Judges penalty submissions having equal votes the convict may choose between these penalties. Convicts may appeal to the Monarchy Crown [Queen Elizabeth II] for Royal Pardon, being up to pardon of up to 1 individual person each week. Obtaining justice shall be free, lawyers

must provide services for free with pay only from a legal aid charity having accreditation to receive donations from 10% levy on home owners income for donation to the earners choices from these charities. Witness including the victim shall receive equal reward for evidence leading to each conviction each month from 1% of the national budget for division equally between each of the 100 local councils for the local court/s each month as compensation and rewards for afflicted for convictions subject to state governor veto of the reward within one month. Black of native ancestry and black citizens born in the Commonwealth nation may get release of prison without welfare into the native title territory area equal to grazing and pastoral lease over an area as the national Parliament shall define of about 10% of the Commonwealth Empire nations land area including adjacent seas to 1 kilometre offshore, Blacks born in our nation may also resettle in local independent nation to receive 10% of the English Commonwealth Empire humanitarian aid budget for equal distribution to the independent nations of (Papua and Mexico) own people including from resettlement of blacks born in our nation and to process illegals who have invaded our fair Commonwealth Empire member nations to return own choice of up to 90% to nation of ancestry regardless of rejection by that country, and to accept the best over 10% as residents for more than 5 years.

83 Royal Tribunal: The Governor General may establish, regulate and appoint and determine terms for investigators, prosecutors and Judges for each Royal Tribunals to pay from Royal Estate with verdicts and penalties subject to Governor General assent the Governor General may have a Royal Tribunal investigate any matter particularly of government if corrupted or disqualified or war crimes done by any personnel within areas of our government and military jurisdiction including in foreign nations who's government by election invites us in alliance coalition to help defend; So not be convicted by our Local Courts. Plus may investigate if was injustice on advice of the Prime Minister.

84 Appeal to Crown [Queen Elizabeth II] for Royal Pardon and also for Referral for (re)-adjudication by voluntary vote by all citizens jurist of all English Commonwealth member nations in council; The English Commonwealth Monarchy Crown [Queen Elizabeth II] may provide 1 Royal Pardon each week for 1 English Commonwealth Empire member nation fair full citizen residing anywhere the English Commonwealth law may have influence, these pardons shall include foreigners the Commonwealth Empire member nation's border protection minister shall choose to exile and banish. The Royal Pardon shall remove and compensate for if wrongly convicted and return confiscated property and fine; This compensation from the agency who wrongly prosecuted shall by GDP divide by population divide by 100 [$700] for each day the wrongly imprisoned or detained and exempt the fair born full citizen from being similarly prosecuted or limited by any person, force, court and tribunal within English Commonwealth Empire jurisdiction and reach and require protection for any similar activity by the fair born citizen so as to be able to continue similar activities subject to annulment by the Monarchy Crown [Queen Elizabeth II] (This 1 Royal Pardon each week for 1 English Commonwealth Empire member nation fair born citizen shall also apply to where living abroad). The English Commonwealth Empire Monarchy Crown [Queen Elizabeth II] may also refer any legal matter in relation to governance, business, religion and charity operations within the English Commonwealth Empire for re-adjudication at the next one month session of the Commonwealth Empire member nations 10 states citizens juries together in tele council.

85 Review of prison and care hospital confinement of citizens such as for if did bad things, if was addicted or if damaged self; Local Courts may impose a penalty if solitary incarceration for free in cell with temperature moderation, shower, toilet and basin with drinking fountain, built in bed with bedding and only true images of self and on television. With provision of food, cleaning and medication needs

(convicts may do cleaning things to earn good behaviour concessions). If the sentence of confinement shall be for more than one year, and one year since the last crime receiving extension of sentence of confinement and one month since damaged self or was addicted to drugs, the care home may release the patient or for convicts the prison shall have the local court review a convicts sentence of confinement. The person in incarceration to offer 1% of savings and welfare Basics Card to the prison island operator charity to spend up to GDP divide by population then divide by 100 [$700] each week to provide after paying for upkeep of the person regular residence have own room with own bathroom, food and essentials and an amount of pay for work as the person is willing so have some freedom or if was not willing let rest in solitary in own room. For convicts on parole free to roam and live on the prison parole island for the remainder of the sentence unless convicted by the Local Court for a crime with a penalty of a term of solitary confinement again with some freedom for productive convict work. Black convicts may at any time obtain banishment to the native title territory area equal to a grazing and cropping lease over an area of about 10% of the Commonwealth Empire member nations lands and adjacent coastal seas to 1 kilometre offshore; To receive equal portion of mining royalties from the native title territory and for our aid blacks may migrate to the independent nations of (Papua and Mexico) to receive 10% of the English Commonwealth Empire humanitarian aid and military budget for people of (Papua and Mexico) to resettle and provide for blacks to freely migrate from any fair English Commonwealth Empire member nation. People who have self harmed or been addicted to drugs which harmed in the last month shall receive visit from free psychiatrist for assessment for free oral medication from 1% of the national budget and maybe compulsory care in hospital where fair full citizens. Health charities to receive 4% levy on home owners income for Health, emergency or disability services charities may include separate hospitals for care if addicted to drugs or if harmed or if damaged self.

People may report overly intoxicated drug addicts including from alcohol who have damaged or humbugged or physically assaulted or endangered or stolen or driven or done any crime to local security police charity. After any criminal conviction during parole offer or any full citizen if wanted so addicted may gain release from confinement to resettle on a prison island in state housing if poor in assets, where may roam free within the coasts of the prison islands free to grow drugs which intoxicated. The prison island operator charity to provide vitals including citizens 3 free welfare ration optimal nutrition bars each day, plus may pay any amount for manual labour when worth while. Former addicted after 1 year free of drugs which harmed by assessment by a free doctor of a drug addict hospital charity having accreditation of the local council for return to civilisation. The national parliament lower first House border protection minister shall determine assessment and detention of for deportation migrants who have done crimes, been problematic or burdened, criminal defence lawyers may not appeal and any suit of behalf of foreigner may not be heard in any court. So enforcement of deportation to the migrants home country of foreign citizenship or main ancestry more than 500 years ago after confinement after the death penalty if repeated savagery or illegally re entered and as additional punishment including to face death penalty from the foreigners own people.

86 Final jurisdiction of Royal Tribunal and Commonwealth Citizens Juries in council: In all matters: (i) arising under any treaty; (ii) affecting consuls or other representatives of other countries; (iii) in which the Commonwealth nation, or a person suing or being sued on behalf of the Commonwealth nation, is a party; (iv)between States, or between residents of different States, or between a State and a resident of another State; (v) in which a writ of prohibition or an injunction is sought against an officer of the Commonwealth nation; the Governor General shall have original jurisdiction through a Royal Court. (vi) Assemblies and Royal tribunals and Constitutional and local courts

(judges and juries) may not accept, read or hear any suit brought on behalf of or any testimony or submission of foreigners or blacks or terrorist dogma. Courts and juries may view photo and silent video of showing criminal activities of foreigners or blacks or terrorists where deleting areas of their writing.

87 Additional final jurisdiction: The Parliament may make laws conferring final jurisdiction to a Royal Tribunal on any matter; (i) arising under this Commonwealth Constitutional FAIR CHARTER, or involving its interpretation; (ii) arising under any laws made by the Parliament;(iii)of military and maritime jurisdiction; (iv) relating to the same subject matter claimed under the laws of different States.

88 Power to define local court jurisdiction: Subject to the above section the Federal Parliament may make laws: (i) defining the additional jurisdictions of any local court having jurisdiction over the local council area; (ii) defining the extent to which the jurisdiction of any local court shall be exclusive; (iii) investing to any of the states local court matters of a State parliament.

89 Proceedings against the Commonwealth nations property including national housing: The Parliament may make laws conferring rights to proceed against the Commonwealth nations property in respect of matters within the limits of the judicial power.

90 Appointment of Local Court Judges and Jurists: Each Local Court room shall have a panel seating 10 judges each of the 10 parties having most citizens born in the local council area as members who shall elect a locally resident member to be Judge in the Local Court until retirement as the Governor General may determine. Each local court shall have 10 jurists from local born able citizen local resident over the age of 20 years of age who voluntarily apply for 1 year, each to have own number to go in lotto ball machine for random appointment as one of 10 Jurists one month in advance for one month and substitutes for if any unable to attend. Indictment or any offence against any local court shall be by jury, and every such trial shall be held in the Local Court of the local council area where the offence

was committed. 80 Remand, convictions and penalties. Local Council shall approve local security police force charities subject to state Governor to arrest criminals until a local judge determines remand and bail terms and date for court appearance the event of multiple judges the higher restriction shall apply. Local security police may not fine or impose any penalty against fair citizens except in self defence and in defence of fair citizens, including of shops, factories and homes. Local Court Conviction shall by on the majority of 11 verdict adding together the verdicts of each of the 10 judges and 10 jurists. Local courts shall have 10 judges The federal jurisdiction of any court may be exercised by such number of judges as the Parliament prescribes. Fair Security Police Officer including border protection shall be able to arrest and deport blacks or illegal invader without access to courts, Send intoxicated, addicts, psychotic or self harmed to hospital confinement or Confine assailants including for illegal supply of drug or intoxicated drivers for trial. Fair security police officers may shoot in defence, in defence of fair citizens, terrorists or fugitive murderers. Property owners including tenants: shall be free to bare common bolt action normal .22 rifles with scope and laser pointer and night vision for to destroy vermin and in self defence only loaded and with ammunition on own property and in defence of fair citizens of our Commonwealth Nation from invasion or to put down government injustice or coup. Segregation of criminals in jail shall be national on basis of gender, race, age and type of crime. All prisoners shall have right to segregation in own cell for own protection and hygiene plus air conditioning for temperature control plus good nutrition health care. All criminals as prisoners shall have sterilisation by a injection after 1 year in prison (cumulative). Worst repeated violent criminals or illegal drug dealers shall have the death penalty at the rate of 1% of criminal prisoners each year. The border protection may deport foreigners who are criminals where this is more severe penalty (including to death penalty) such as in exchange for return of Australians, to save money or where imprisonment has been used as a way for foreigners to obtain extended residency with free protection, food, care and perks or as a way to spread terrorist religion.

Chapter IV—Finance

100 Consolidated Revenue Fund: All revenues or moneys raised or received by the Governments of the Commonwealth nation shall form one Consolidated Revenue Fund, for the Federal parliament to appropriated including in the national budget for local and state government subject to the English Commonwealth FAIR CHARTER.

101 Tax collection: All tax collection and levy distribution management shall be automatic by the persons Bank (to keep 1% of taxes and levies) having approval of the Federal Parliament. No obligation on anybody to lodge tax forms.

102 Money to be appropriated by law: No money shall be drawn from the Treasury of the Commonwealth except under appropriation originating with the Federal Parliaments Prime Ministers Treasurer minister such as in the annual budget.

103 Transfer of Local and State governments departments and public servants to Federal Parliament: On any on transfer of a department of the public service of a State becomes transferred to the Federal Parliament the employment of all existing public servants of the department shall be subject to a Prime Ministers minister; With all property of any kind exclusively in connection with the department, the Federal Parliament may acquire any property of any kind in use, but not exclusively by the department without compensation to the state, minister shall on transfer, assume responsibility for regulations of the department.

104 Use of taxes revenues: 40% of revenue of our nation shall be for Federal Parliament to allocate to the states and local councils in proportion to population originating with the Prime Ministers Treasurers. 40% of revenue shall be for welfare. 20% shall be for English Commonwealth Military. All for expenditure in the English Commonwealth Nation on local recipients.

105 Budget portion for states: During a period of ten years after the

establishment of the Commonwealth and thereafter until the Parliament otherwise provides, of the net revenue of the Commonwealth from duties of customs and of excise not more than one fourth shall be applied annually by the Commonwealth towards its expenditure. Surplus shall go to political parties in proportion to the number of members having election to government assembly (Local, State and Federal assemblies)

106 Consistent taxation and rates: One single rate of 50% tax on exodus currency from the English Commonwealth and of tariffs of each member nation on importation of products also made in the nation. All taxes, fees, fines and levies, plus all utilities rates per unit of usage shall be the same across the 10 states of the nation subject he English Commonwealth FAIR CHARTER. No tax shall exist on transfer of assets including people, information and money between the 10 states of the nation.

107 States Business Council: The states 100 largest private businesses by revenue in the state for which all 10 directors reside in the same state. Each of the 10 largest share holders shall appoint 1 director: To: approve: 100 unregulated private boarding schools in the state to receive the proceeds of levies on all sales.

108 Consistent subsidies for production and export: The Reserve Bank shall issue new currency as a 25% subsidy on each payment transaction for exports for portion grown and made in our English Commonwealth nation as the bank shall administer (except not for wild sea-foods and finite essential resources).

109 Local supply and properties to be off-grid: All local energy shall be from as local sources as possible and from within the Commonwealth Nation. All homes shall be single story (except for state capital city square mile), be 100% off grid having Wireless communications, Free eternal effortless electricity including for air-conditioning, Rainwater tanks with inflow filters and outflow pumps and recycling of water for automatic irrigation of nutritional food species such as plants and trees, Pit toilet with fumes treatment via

exhaust fan, All products and packaging (housing may endure) must be combustible, non toxic and quickly bio degrade in sea water or if toxic have no cost disposal of product at end of life. For each bedroom the new single story home shall on more than one quarter hectare of land and each home shall have enough back yard to be able to feed 1+ chickens without purchase of feed. Local data centres shall be local more than 100m underground and more than 100m above sea level. All communications, banking and energy systems shall be able to survive x60 electromagnetic storms and if having had failed electrical grid.

110 Local Councils: Local fair citizens shall elect to each of the 10 local councils of each state 20 members from the local council area to elect a Mayor as Speaker, being 1 male and 1 female from each of the 10 local council area divisions. The local council shall vote to: (i) Approve big constructions subject to the Governor Generals choice of general plan; (ii) Approve 100 charities for the local council area from which property owners to pay 10% levy on personal incomes to own choices of local charities ; (ii) Commission local private businesses and charities to repair and maintain local infrastructure and natural environment remove rubbish or pollution including bulky rubbish and toxic waste from near the front door for free on call; (iii) From local fair citizens born in the local council area members of the local council to elect representatives: 5 male and 5 female local fair citizens to the first lower house (the house of assembly) of the State Parliament and 1 male and 1 female to the first lower house (the house of common representatives) of the federal national parliament.

111 States: Each of the 10 states of the English Commonwealth nation 10 local councils shall elect and within each 3 years as the Mayor determines 5 male and 5 female fair born all 100 year ancestry citizens to the 100 members first house (the lower house of assembly) of the state parliament. The Governor shall employ and pay from the Royal Estate an organisation to each month randomly select from willing fair citizens born in the state: 100 to be members of the state Citizens Jury

for each month. The State House of Assemble shall legislate and reform the states current model English Commonwealth Constitutional FAIR CHARTER to put to all state Citizens Juries in the English Commonwealth each month. The Citizens Jury shall vote to appoint a Speaker and consider video conference debates, from all state citizens juries in the Fair English Language Commonwealth Empire: To as a whole in the first week vote to rank model Fair English Language Commonwealth Empire Constitutional FAIR CHARTER submissions from all states lower houses, in the second week vote to approve or reject the leading FAIR CHARTER model subject to Crown [Queen Elizabeth II] assent, in the third week vote to approve or reject the Fair English Language Commonwealth Empires military Presidents defence budget and policy update, and in the forth week of the month vote on each member nations from each of the state Governors a choice of 1 judicial case, and if the Presidents defence budget and policy update failed to pass in the last week votes on candidates for President of the military in two rounds with a run off of the two leading by votes in the first round over 3 days in the second round over 2 days.

112 Distribution of budget surplus: Budget surplus shall go to parties in proportion to members in parliament for equal payment to public servants in the employment of a minister subject to Prime Ministers approval.

113 Customs duties: A tax of 50% shall apply on the exodus of all currency from the English Commonwealth such as to buy imported product, avoided tax or squeezed workers. An additional tariff of 50% shall apply on any product category for which the Commonwealth nation produces a replacement. The Commonwealth nation may not apply tariffs to individual foreign companies. The federal parliament shall apply a levy per kilogram (as part of the tax on the weight of exports) of products sourced from living nature such as seafood and timber for seeding and replenishment of these species.

114 Financial assistance to States and Local Councils: The federal

parliament shall provide money to States and Local council areas of equal amount per (fair population x area in hectares)

115 Audit: 1% of revenues of businesses, charities, parliaments, royal estate, military budget, and local councils shall be for audit as the Governor General determines.

116 International agreements: May only about communications, medication, military, electrical power and navigation standards. All genes and standards such as in medications and technologies are free to copy. International agreements are subject to ongoing assent of the English Commonwealth Crown [Queen Elizabeth II] and the federal national Parliaments and may be broken with all penalties or charges void.

117 Federal national parliament may not allocate to a particular state, region and local council: The Federal Parliament shall not make allocation to a particular state, region and local council, Only to all states, regions and local councils in proportion to (population x area in hectares). The state and local council shall spend monies by spending submissions (so each has a total value of over GDP / population) subject to veto by the vote of 100 senators, and military by spending submission subject to veto by the Commonwealth nations Governor General.

118 No cost on the right to use own water: Property owners shall have the right to free use of water falling on own land and under own land. The State Parliament shall determine management of state rivers, storm water recycling, desalination. All homes shall have 5000litre rainwater tank/s per bedroom with filter and pump. The Federal parliament shall determine management of rivers crossing state borders for water quality and irrigation.

119 Inter-State Planning Commission: The Governor-General shall have Inter-State Infrastructure Planning Commission to plan infrastructure including across state borders.

120 States Parliaments with assent of the state Governor may modify or withdraw from or part from the inter-state infrastructure plan within

own state.

121 Inter-State Planning Commissioners' appointment, tenure, and remuneration: The members of the Inter State Planning Commission: (i) shall be by appointment by the Governor General in council with state Governors each advancing candidates for 1 commissioner; (ii) shall hold office for up to seven years, but may be removed within that time by the Governor General such as on the ground of misbehaved or incapacitated; (iii) each shall receive such remuneration from the Royal Estate as the Governor General determines; but such remuneration shall not be diminished during the commissioners times on this commission; (iv) the Reserve Bank shall issue new currency for state commissioner to commission the construction of free national housing for the Royal Estate to back the national currency and so all fair full citizens of more than 100 years ancestry in the state of the Fair English Language Commonwealth Empire Nation in last 200 years adding together lineages if poor in assets shall have single story off grid quiet national housing (more than 100m from a main road). To pay rent of 20% of income including welfare as rent, the first GDP/population, then /500 [$140] per week going to the housing provider and manager such as the charity, school and bank. Not for illegals we have invaded our nation such as fugitives or dark people (natives shall get native title over 10% of the nations land area)

122 Saving of certain rates; Nothing in this Constitution shall render unlawful any rate for the carriage of goods upon a railway, the property of a State, if the rate is deemed by the Inter State Commission to be necessary for the development of the territory of the State, and if the rate applies equally to goods within the State and to goods passing into the State from other States.

123 Payments and debts: All payment where possible shall be in advance such as by escrow. Budget allocations shall be a percentage of revenue and may only be spent when in account. Payment to suppliers shall be in advance of supply (escrow), on supply the buyer may release payment, after a period in the agreement where still in

escrow either party may take the payment to the local court to recover, Unpaid government debts including government debts shall be void and default after the presenting of the general budget (near the end of the financial year), Except health shops chains (having approval of the federal health minister and local council) may issue credit and only for care and medical treatments to default at death, Health shops may refuse credit for expensive treatments to people with large debts or expected death, If a minister has a run a deficit the minister shall go to prison until no longer a minister then 1day for every GDP/population of debt. Government's, businesses, businesses and individuals may rent out goods, Charities may only give and lend out items in exchange after donation of an equal weight of good acceptable items such as of clothes, furniture and machinery (not money) where donation of good acceptable items to the charity (by weight) must be in advance of delivery of items to the person in need. All new financial debts are illegal and void after 1 year. People may spend one year as a convict in free solid community service to void own other material or service debts. 1% of the parliament and local council budget revenue and the all of the budget surplus since the presentation of the last budget to the presentation of the next budget shall go to parties in proportion to popular vote at general election for payment by party leaders to ministers choice of staff and public servants subject to approval of the Prime Minister.

Chapter V—The States

133 State Constitutions and legislation: The Constitution and legislation of each State of the Commonwealth shall, subject to this Federal legislation, continue as is and shall only update by the state parliament to be in compliance with the Prime Ministers choice of Fair English Language Commonwealth Empire Constitutional FAIR CHARTER update.

134 Secession: States may not secede unless on a separate land mass area (island) or with own predominate other language by 60% majority referendum of full fair citizens with 100+ year ancestry

(adding together lineages) on that land mass or language area in the last 200 years.

135 Saving of State laws: Every law in force in a Colony which to becomes a State, and relating to any matter within the powers of the Parliament of the Commonwealth, shall, subject to this Constitution, continue in force in the State; and, until provision is made in that behalf by the Parliament of the Commonwealth and the Parliament of the State so as to be in compliance with the Prime Ministers choice of more recent Fair English Commonwealth Constitutional FAIR CHARTER update (having valid approval of the Citizens Jury and Monarchy as Crown [Queen Elizabeth II]).

136 Inconsistency of laws: The law of a State shall apply except where inconsistent with a law of the Federal national parliament, in which case the latter shall prevail, and the former shall, to the extent of the inconsistency, be void.

137 State Governor: The Governor General shall appoint and replace the Governor of each State direct the Governor.

138 State surrender of territory to another adjoining state: The Parliament of a State may surrender any part of the State including islands to an adjoining State of the Fair English Language Commonwealth Empire nation with English Commonwealth Crown [Queen Elizabeth II] assent.

139 State inspection laws: States parliaments may require free quarantine inspections and referral to local courts. Plus monitor, catch, apprehend, punish and deport immediately illegal blacks who have invaded or terrorised the state even if having obtained citizenship as with border protection.

140 Intoxication: Beverages and foods may be up to 6% alcohol and shall come with 1km taxi voucher for each 10ml of alcohol. Various cannabis oils and powder drinks are subject to 90% drug sales levy to pay to a rehab hospital (instead of paying all sales levy) such as from basics card (no Medicare rebate subsidy to pharmacy unless under prescription) as available at rehab clinic from local health shop via

rehab clinic having approval of the local council such as for pain, nausea, epilepsy, ex drug addicts, spasms or cancer where the user having replacement of their driver license with an intoxicants user license who may be subject to confinement at the rehab clinic such as on island for convicts or addicted. All other intoxicants may only be grown or sold as the convict of addicted island charity operator rehab clinic determines subject to 90% levy on sales for the rehab clinic.

141 Local fair citizens security police, emergency services and militia forces: Local council shall approve fair security police, emergency services and militia forces charities to have volunteers who may bare arms within the local council area to keep fair citizens safe. These charities to receive portion of 10% levy on property owners incomes for earners choices from 100 charities having approval of the local council.

142 National Commerce and Currency: BANKS: Issue of the new only valid general national electronic currency shall be only by 10 private banks (to only do money management) with each state business council approving 1 bank each, subject to approval, investigation and disciplines of governor generals royal tribunals. These banks may operate in any state and country, Each resident and citizen shall only have one bank account at only one of these 10 private banks (plus may use independent payment processing services). These banks shall for customers manage and issue standard valid crypro-currency, Subject to a 20% tax on withdrawal as matte gold and matte silver 1oz and 1/10oz coins plus 1% fee for the automatic teller machine provider. The cash economy is free of sales levies and same currency transaction taxes where within the Fair English Language Commonwealth Empire nation, In this free local physical gold and silver coin economy, all of each merchants coinage at the end of each week over GDP/population/10 [$7,000] x number the number of the merchants contiguous shop properties must go into any one of the 10 banks who may hold any amount of coinage. Shops may keep change in line with openly written store policy. Only health

shops may provide (free) credit and only on and for purchase for health products and treatments. Electronic transactions require a live video photo plus bio-metric identification card, plus upload of photo of the account holder to the merchants terminal from the account holders bank (which the merchant may keep on record for future transactions), plus entry of the account holders pin. Each local council area shall have 10 roundish suburbs/counties of about equal population. Each bank must have a branch in one suburb/county in each local council area so as not to establish a branch in a district where any of the 10 banks has an active branch (so as to have branches across the local council area). Bank branches shall also function as local basics card welfare assessment offices. Small town banks may also have a postal service franchise for parcel customs, holding and postage franchise. All housing foreclosures must be for private royal estate national socialist housing for the subsequent 20 years after the foreclosure as with Royal Estate national state housing for rent to homeless fair good citizens of the commonwealth nations having 100+ years ancestry adding together lineages in last 200 years if asset poorest, for the tenant to pay 20% of income (including of welfare) as rent, the first to GDP/population/500 [$140] each week to the housing provider and manager, the remainder surplus rent to go to into the national budget. Plus 10% of income (including of welfare) for the tenant to accumulate for the tenant to spend on future maintenance and improvements of the tenants residence wherever will reside and to use to purchase own land and own home construction. ISSUE OF NEW CURRENCY: Each of these 10 banks may issue new crypto-currency as follows: (but not for lending); 1% x GDP each year for to commission construction of Royal Estate national state housing to be off grid, quiet, single story housing for fair full citizens having 100 years ancestry in the state of the fair English Language Fair Commonwealth nation in last 200 years adding together lineages if homeless poor in assets (at schools for children and students, military and if poor in assets: veterans and descendants of patriots who have fallen in the line of duty, charity volunteers, public servants and knowledge workers and for hospitals if homeless hospitals including from domestic violence, addicted and prisons if a convict. Plus in Papua and Mexico for processing of all and for resettlement of some illegals who have invaded. To have own bedroom (cost of ~GDP/population x 5 per bedroom). For tenants to pay 20% of income as rent, with the first GDP/population/500 [$140] each week to the provider and manager. 10% of income for the tenant to save and spend on future maintenance and improvements of the tenants residence wherever will reside, also for moving services, loan furniture, linen, electrical and appliances, plus for maintenance services such as front garden and lawn care, repair, painting, security and excess goods or rubbish removal. An amount of GDP/population/100 [$700] per week at (from) each bio-metric identification self adding crypto-currency Basics Card productive full citizens if poor in assets (see powers of the national parliament); 20% subsidy to exporters for valid national currency inflows from exports from the fair English Language Fair Commonwealth Nation in proportion to costs of production in the same fair English Commonwealth nation for payment for currency inflows from outside of the fair English Commonwealth area into a bank in the fair English Commonwealth nation; Local food growers subsidy GDP / population / 20,000 [$3.50] x kg for farmer grown medicinal, nutritional and timber content of plant, tree, fungus, microbe, wool (to shear in spring), egg and milk produce (not for meat, bone, water, bad fat or simple sugar content) subsidy for the farmer only for produce for products for human consumption. Not paid for water content or waste, The subsequent food maker, furniture maker, builder and merchant must repay subsidy for produce wasted or disposed of; For each full citizens (after 20 years probationary residency) guarantee of unit deposits in one the 10 official banks in the same fair English Commonwealth nation to recover the accounts deposit unit value losses against the value of gold and silver after the end of the calendar year of up to GDP/population/10 for each full citizen for the year including personal private and personal business accounts losses in deposits unit value. COMMERCE: Merchants selling from the Fair English Language Commonwealth Empire nation may only accept the official national crypto-currency as payments as deposits in the same nation. Banks shall not interfere with the value of the currency. Deposit interest rates are not set and shall be as the gain or loss in the conversion rate of the national currency and the conversion value of units of in the banks single shares fund with immediate access for transfer, withdrawal and spending from the unit account of up to 10% of deposits each day plus as the bank approves for spending in the national currency at the unit value at the time of the withdrawal and spending being total market value of all of the shares in the fund divided equally by all units in the fund to only list in ordinary shares in business listing on official share markets in the same fair English Commonwealth nation and where the business to buy shares in has more than 50% of total assets existing in the same fair English Commonwealth nation. All of the banks own, the banks directors (one director for each of the 10 share holders owning most shares), the banks staff, and the banks share transaction decisions staff financial assets as the same units in the same fund with the same bank, With the bank to receive each month 1/1000 x total units in the fund as new units as payment. All of the funds investment gains or losses go to the deposit holders as unit holders. Peer to peer transactions and balance records ledger update and verification to 100 largest branch data centres verifying so updating each other. Deposits in the fair English Commonwealth nations digital currency, may transfer tax free on to the bank account holders tax free Basics (copy proof) Micro-SD digital wallet also with deposit balance, transaction history, bio-metric identity profile, ten last transaction photo, 10 3D recognition photo models, medical records, DNA test genetics profile (racial origins or susceptibilities) medical directives, end of life euthanasia directives, accounts access such for (phone, utility and rent of providers having approval of the welfare minister with a special password for each

biller which the card owner may cancel), current medical, citizenship status, visas, full name, name at birth, place of birth, date of birth, citizenship of parents, ancestry, children, passport, licenses (alcohol and driving), drug consumption, drinker status, mental health status, next of kin to inherit, will, occupation (may self edit), criminal records including confinement status, area access, and passwords (with 4 digit pin, 16 digit master account management password, 16 digit bank access password and 16 digit individual long random passwords) such to put in phones, smart watches, pendants and smart cards with display, For tax free purchase of essentials having approval of the minister, including with self adding of appropriate welfare payments. With peer to peer transaction cross verification between local merchant and when able upload of transaction information to the bank to limit fraud. Merchants must have a standard electronic point of sale device. The merchant must also see the photo identification on the merchant device from the Micro-SD such as via a phone, smart watch, pendant and smart card also with pin and electronic camera image feed recognition verification with image recognition optional for in store purchasers and merchant platforms having approval and trust of the banking minister. The currency unit account owner may authorises generation of a special password to allow each merchant such as landlord to receive payments from the account owners account. Shops in our nation may use wireless digital price tags showing the price linking to the payment, inventory and product bar-code system of the store to automatically update the tag by secure wireless. Media transactions subject to digital rights management protocol. Only local health shops having approval of the health minister may provide debt and only for nutritional medicine. Debt may not be used to purchase established housing, debt (from
overseas) may be used for new construction, renovation, production equipment or seed. Only savings, up to 30% of the account holders future income/revenue (total adding together and paying first obligations only) for up to 50years, set levels of quantitative easing

and foreign debt may finance such as for construction and production machinery. Finance and lending providers may not foreclosure during the life of the purchaser where able to make payments, then only for to be permanent national housing for homeless asset-poor citizens paying 20% of gross income and each month, plus 10% of the tenants gross income for the tenant to save for maintenance at any property the tenant will rents. The tenant may leave at any time without penalty. If a tenant is evicted (such as by a new owner) the owner must pay compensation of GDP/population/5 [$14,000] to the head tenant for moving expenses. Property owners may sell the property (with tenant to continue in place) and only on open market with proceeds to first repay original debts for the occupants purchase of the property for the seller then owing nothing. Property may not be collateral for other debt. Financial debts (including of governments or to foreign places) shall be void at the end of each year. No fee or obstacle may be put on early payment, change of address and transfer between service providers. Banks may issue replacement currency for currency damaged or destroyed. Any biller may be blocked at any time by any account holder. All account holders must nominate beneficiaries to transfer deposits to after dormant for 5 years. Each citizens accounts in one of the 10 banks in our nation may be overdrawn by up to GDP/population/100 [$700] with no fees but the bank may block transactions while account is negative. BUSINESSES AND SHARE MARKETS: Establishment of and investment in any business shall not be restricted by regulation. Banks shall register any personal business (subject to criminal record check) on minimum deposit a single amount set by the bank into a business account and also the business property within the bank account for the bank to manage automatic taxation with a unique company name not elsewhere used in the last 50 years taking up to 1 day for approval. Personal business are the account owners property (not of the spouse) and only pass to children at death as inheritance. Shares listing on a share market having approval of the banking minister may issue (sell) shares only at market price where above book value per share (half years revenue plus half cost of assets). On subsequent transfer sale of shares (only at market prices on the share market) the seller shall pay 30% of proceeds to the underlying business and 3% of the proceeds to the share market platform. 10% of listing business revenue shall go to weekly tax free dividend to each share for the shareholders to accumulate until the share holder is able to purchase additional shares in the same business. Business may never de-list from an official share market and may never be removed from listing on the same share market while in existence until after this share market has ceased to operate in the fair English Commonwealth nation. All businesses shall pay 1% of revenue as a tax free dividend to the founder during the life of the founder and then to charities having approval of a local council. All businesses listing in the fair English Commonwealth nation shall have 10 directors, each a full citizen of this nation (after 20 years probationary residency) with each of the 5 largest share holder by ordinary shares to appoint and replace 1 female director and 1 male director. Director may only be director of 1 business at a time and may not be paid or be rewarded or receive any benefit from any-entity or any-one except any amount may be paid by the top share holder (one of top 5) as the directors employer. All derivatives or financial instruments where the share holder has not own the underlying business asset or having the potential for more than 100% loss of the cash investment are illegal and void. Share market prices shall go up to 3 digit numerals (above zero). Each trader may have up to 10 free purchase bids and sell offer price orders at any one time, for any duration only subject to cancellation by the trader, which may be at any price, subject to 1 day delay for where over 10% either side of the current market price. The trader may sell all shares at market price of within 1% either side of price when placing sell order, Also the trader may specify a number of shares to sell and at when at what price. Any person and entity including any foreigner may also buy and hold shares on the fair English Commonwealth nations official share markets. Only full citizens (after 20 years probationary and ancestral residency) and business listing on an official share market in the fair English Commonwealth nation may buy more than 1 hectare of property and constructions with prior owners (foreigners may commission construction and then own constructions on up to 1hectare of land). Brokerage fees to the bank share market trading web-page, registry and platform are market set. Companies, shares broker and shares registry may not send paper mail to share holder. Traders of business who have deceived other investors such as to prospects, revenues, profits and assets or for insider trading is subject to ban for 1-10 years as a local court shall determine. All share traders must disclose why the trader is choosing to buy, hold and sell each business share for automatic display to all for more than 1 day prior to placing the order, without disclosing quantity to buy and sell. For access by any investor looking up the profile on the business. Investor may list market depth list of buyers and sellers with the investors identity and this note. Traders market information and live market information including market prices and depth must be available free to all. For bids beginning at above the market price of above 1% of the shares in the business investments, no other trader may lodge a higher bid until this order is fully met until/unless the trader cancels the order for shares in the order yet to have. No one including broker may track investor on-line activity for insider trading (tracked what shares the investor is looking at to purchase or sell before the investor is able to get the order, But the observer may not know current orders of any other investor but may buy a holding in the same shares as the other investor after full execution and reporting of the other investors buy order, with permission from the investor friends may buy and sell own shares after the original investor gets own order through. Shares may not be sold at a loss except to liquidate estate of deceased investor if required: share holders may not sell shares under the purchase price of the same shares. All share holdings and investments and all other assets of all investors and citizens of our nation are available for free access by all including for automatic welfare assets test and taxes assessment. Share may only sell at above intrinsic value per share (50% book value + 50% of last years product sales revenue)/share. The listing share market platform organisation must have over 100 audit reporting accountant firm and appoint 2 auditor replacing 1 each year with a new auditor so as each auditor has a 2 years within the last 10 years. The auditor to weekly update sales, assets and all information relevant market to all with minimal burden to the company (market prices and depth and traders notes run by the share market platform operator). No entity may take over or acquire more than 20% of shares in a listing company, the board may not cancel or transfer shares or sell more than 10% of in use production assets each year. TRADE WITHIN THE 10 STATES (of the fair English Commonwealth nation shall be absolutely free, except in matters of state customs controls for quarantine and prevention of entry of criminals or illegal foreign migrants or illegal weapons or illegal drugs. The national parliament not to give preference. The National Parliament shall not, by any law or regulation of trade, commerce, or revenue, give preference to one State or any part thereof over another State or any part thereof. Laws with respect to navigation, or shipping, airlines, and railway carriers shall be made by the national parliament. LOCAL FARMING: The top 10 local farmers by production in the local council district shall each have 1 director on board of 10 to make food product purchasing decisions for the top 2 local supermarkets from 60% of the supermarkets food sales. (Health shops having approval of the local council and health minister may make own health product purchase decisions. With 3 free optimal nutrient welfare ration bars each day for citizens as want these as the national Health minister and parliament commission with local ingredients) Supermarket business owners such as for chain the board of 10 shareholder board make all additional purchasing and pricing decisions. The biggest local council area groceries supermarket by sales in the last year including online shopping distribution warehouses must provide free stocking while having room on delivery of all long life food grown in the state for free to receive payment only after sale of the long life produce to consumers for the price set by the distributor to only get payment within one month after the sale of produce to consumers and for the grower farmer to get 60% of sale proceeds (before home delivery), the processor, packers, transporter, distributor and supermarket retailer working out how to cut 40%. For fresh produce with production subsidy on sale by the farmer, for sale to consumers within 1 week of picking, laying and milking, after which the fresh produce shall be free to the poor in food-bank section of the seller for 1 week, then disposed with the merchant repaying the production subsidy (where farmer selling the produce cancelled subsidy). Each farm may process own produce and sell produce direct to consumers, processors, packagers, wholesalers and retailers. Merchants may only own 1 farm. On-line groceries such as supermarket distribution warehouses must list all produce by unit price of actually produce not including the container, in consistent unit of per kilogram. Merchants such as supermarkets may not import food, Individuals as end consumers (including for family) may import food tax free such as vitamin and complementary medicine supplements only from within the fair English Commonwealth nations. {Commonwealth Empire}. All animal products must go through an official process before contact and consumption by end consumers such as cooking and pasteurisation for colostrum products though a special process which will not destroy immunity boosting factors such as immunoglobulins. Families may produce and drink and eat own raw egg and milk products such as cows milk only where from the families own animals not mixed with milk and egg from more than one animal and bird. Chemical pesticides or herbicides are illegal only pest genome specific biological controls such as infections to at genes specific to the pest add genes to make contraceptives and physical destruction such as by electrocution, natural predators, fencing, fast lethal traps, robot, weeding, ploughing and shooting and nutrient and health positive pungent herbal deterrents controls and elimination may exist. Crops may not have herbicide resistance and may be bred for herbicide susceptibility for emergency control of infestations in quarantine. SHOP RETAIL TENANCIES: business renting shops such as for manufacture, repair and retailers shall pay 10% of revenue to shop owner/s. Shop owners shall give 1 years notice on free rent if shop tenancy is terminated. POSTAL SERVICES (and local post office franchise): Postal franchise must home deliver to homes and businesses in the same fair English Commonwealth nation for a basic single amount per delivery, plus an amount per delivery for each overseas area and to foreign nation post office (may include home delivery as available) x distance between the land area of the sender and the land area of the recipient (no extra charge for within the senders same land area and nation), plus an amount per gram (dividing by 5 for weights over 1kg); for delivery to within 5 kilometres of one of the 10 banks post office as local postal franchises holder, to the mail box on the recipients property for small items and to the front door on the recipients property for larger items up to 10kg. The nearest postal franchise holder/s as having approval of the local council shall have responsibility for and collect mail from local postal boxes and facilities for to send and receive mail. Additional postal services shall include unregulated same rate per kilobyte pay digital mail for delivery by satellite TV and mobile phones and wireless internet towers. Of postal service physical mail and parcel delivery charges 25% for senders post office for collection, sender services, processing and sorting for correct postal services, 25% for the postal service for collection from senders post offices and moving mail and parcels to receivers post offices, 25% of postal rates for additional mail collection, sorting and long distance transport contractor, and 25% for the receivers post office to deliver to the recipients property.

143 Religion: The populist democratic Federal Parliament may ban any religion that has abused or terrorised including all books, places of

worship or symbols and jailing and expulsion of their fanatics. Our parliaments and local councils may each legislate additional rules and observances without ceding power to any other religion. People in our Commonwealth nation may only swear in on the Christian holy Bible and Jewish Torah. Commonwealth nations governments, prisons, schools, public servants, charities, children and migrants shall be, respect and observe books and constructive traditions of constructive of Christian and Jewish religions including in Sundays 1 hour listening to live guidance and only cleaning and good deeds without pay. All religions are subject to the Commonwealth nations populist democratic Commonwealth FAIR CHARTER and Constitution law enforcement. Only Christian Churches and Jewish Synagogues may exist in our Commonwealth nation as places of worship, attendance for good citizens shall be voluntary. Good productive fair full citizens shall have free will to create own religion, observance and model policy submissions. Books and preaching of religion shall include metaphoric analogy to demonstrate morel principles, subject to correction by the living leader of the religion to be non fiction in light of the progress of science. The chief Jewish Rabbi in Jerusalem may edit, update and print the Jewish Torah. Only the current Pope in Vatican City may edit , update and print the Holy Christian Bible after vote of the Popes choice of fair cardinals each born in a separate country. No person may force anyone to do or submit to anything that violates Jewish and Christian traditions and texts subject to this English Commonwealth FAIR CHARTER. +Commandments and directives: Thou shall not kill except to save good fair true Christian and Jewish life; Thou shall not worship reverse or virtual or cartoon or single reflection mirror images; Thou shall only contemplate designs and true images of self and world such as on television, video and reflection of reflection at slightly acute of right angle in corner; General natural life plan; Thou men shall Serve and learn from your father to age 25 years, Research, volunteer for nation and fight others from 25 years of age to 50 years of age, Grow, make, build and sell things from 50 years of age to 75 years of age and Have, teach and discipline children from 75years of age to 100years of age; Thou girls shall go to school and learn to 25years of age, Have children, marry and care for family from 25years to 50years of age, Care for disabled from 50years of age to 75years of age, Teach and guide spiritually from 75years to 100years of age. Thou shall require male homosexuals to obtain a license for homosexual activity from a local court including for homosexual propaganda; Thou shall put evil in the past and make the future good; Thou shall not be in debt and shall condemn debtors; Thou shall have non biological dwellings except shall have biological doors, floors, window frames and furniture. Roof shall be metal and walls shall be stone, brick or concrete on steal frame; Thou shall have rest from physical work every second day and do only free charity work on Sundays. Females shall celebrate December as Christmas by giving gifts of food, Men shall celebrate December as Christmas by giving free samples of work; Thou shall have male priests in marriage union as master with his wife a female priest as servant; Thou shall have 10+ food produce trees and 1+ egg layer for food for each family member; Thou shall eat unprocessed food, vitamins and supplements; Thou shall not deploy toxic chemicals such as agricultural pesticides or domestic bug spray and shall not insert toxic chemical genes in food and shall have biological, contraceptive and physical control of pests; Thou shall be in shade from sun while having face and hands visible as much as possible; Thou shall wear locally made clothes and eat locally grown food and buy buy locally made products; Thou shall not wear high or narrow heels or wear make up or spray tan or camouflage paint; Thou and family shall save money and treat own illnesses or injury and shall not partake of socialised medicine or medical insurance; Thou shall grow only productive species, such as to produce food; Thou shall have fair white orange complexion and be nude of face hair and blue eyes, males shall have bald scalp and black body hair, females shall be nude of body hair and have yellow blonde scalp hair; Thou shall favour fair

Christians and Jewish charity for who have stopped giving for financial reasons over those who have never given; Thou shall only have fair Christian and Jewish migrants, houses of worship and books and exile all other blacks, migrants of bad religions or fugitives who have invaded and flatten their places of worship, verbally vilify them and burn their books; Thou shall not normally eat meat at home, only away from home or in emergencies, (bone and joint powder and eggs and milk always okay). The meaning (purpose) of life is to mate female beauty with male longevity. How to think and communicate for optimal results; basically talk about bad problems of past and good solutions for future, more in depth; talk about alternatives of; Good/positive adjectives/yes/idea/peace/surplus/allow/thanks; about; Future We-me-i You-truth teller Truth Profit True image selfie/video Design Crops/livestock White Police Creative Nutritional Healthy Productive Successful Energy And When Local Agreement Populist democracy. Yes about true, ok about good future. Bad/negative adjectives/no-not-don't/aggression/deficit/avoid/sorry;-about; Past Them You-liar, Fiction words Debt Reverse image reflection Art Wild species Black Crime Destruction Toxicity Illness Bum Failure Lethargy Or/But/Except If Foreign Disagreement Tyranny. No/not about false or bad or past. Current time about relationship, alliance, sex: also abilities and needs status update reports. Truth about any time events where having photographic evidence including of a future and about natural geographical and weather events of any time such as forecasting and natural scientific truths of any time..... Have only true image of self for self control: join 2x 2meter tall x 7cm wide mirrors by tape up outside of junction. Have these 2 mirrors at slightly acute of right angle so as to have 2 true images of self central on each side when viewing from middle of room. Have two of these in the opposite corner of the room for additional self defence capabilities. Record self saying all combination of phonetics alphabet pairs (42 x 42 = 1764 transitions) while between these live true images of self, and listen to when on computer between these live true image of self and with a true image pair in corner opposite a television when watching television (through the true image pairs in corner to wake up, filter, focus and set goals). Have a shield from reverse images on each side wall such as tall cupboards and shelves. Have television and computer monitor opposite these true image reflection of reflection corner mirror pairs. Present only own best true images, voice and texts to world. (normal reverse images of single reflection mirror have caused self destructive confused behaviour or lied).

ALPHABET; Vowels to be round font symbols and consonants to be strait font symbols;

VOWELS;
6 Short;

At	gEt	It	On	Up	bOOk

ɑ ɛ ɩ o ʋ ü

6 Mid;

hARd	AIr	tURn	fOR	EAr	hOW

α ☉ ℥ ↄ ⍵ ⍵

6 Long;

sAY	bEE	EYE	gO	tOO	bOY

Λ Ɛ Θ Ω ⍵⍵ ⍵⍵

Lorris Harmlawf;

LOΓΓɩΣ HαMLɔF

CONSONANTS;
6 Throat;

Has	kiNG	Roy	Yes	Get	King

H Ͷ Γ Y G K

6-Back of tongue and pallet;

CHip	Jug	viSion	SHe	Zap	Set

⊏ ⊐ Ж Ш Z Σ

6 Mid to front of tongue and pallet;

No	Do	Lid	Top	THe	THin

N D L T ħ π

6 Lips and teeth;

Vote	Find	We	My	Be	Post

V F W M ь P

HUMAN NAMING CODE;

Man own first name; consonants;

1st only front, 2nd only throat, 3rd not back, 4th not lips; vowels first only short, last only short.

Girl own first name; consonants;

1st not throat, 2nd only back, 3rd not lips, 4th only front; vowels first only long, last only long.

Last surname; consonants;

1st only throat, 2nd only lips, 3rd not back, 4th not front; vowels first only mid, last only mid.

[Note; for human names; First letter throat consonants for men; turning bad into good, bravery, quiet, kindness, caring, honesty, sympathy, freedom, pleasantness and service to self in broader sense so may include saving whole world for own benefit. First letter lips consonants for women for passion, strict, discipline, clean and service to community for reward from community. Throat consonants for women; slack, lazy, insane, covert treachery, fragile, reckless, undisciplined or careless. Lips consonants first for men; were enraged, deceived, misrepresented, demented, dogmatic, harsh, destructive, cowardly, deviantly swindled, buggered, raped, traitor, intruded, imposed, enslaved, abused, stressed. Second consonant throat consonants for calm; (lips consonants for second letter were paranoid)

Third consonant same as second consonant. Forth consonant back of tongue and pallet for men; loyal, patriotic, populist, protective, intelligence, persistent, learning, pragmatic, technological, fair, just, decisive. These names 8 consonants also seem to correspond to decades of average 80 years of human lifespan. Fifth consonants throat for mental inventiveness, intuitive and leadership and lips physically creative employee. Sixth consonants lips for soldier, throat for creator. Seventh consonants throat for soldier, lips for creator.

Eighth consonant at end of surname lips for wealthy and dominant, throat for was poor or submissive. Apparently order in name signify time process order with starting position first letters with h being to transform from bad to the result to the last letter with p being good for females good p to better p.

Outlook; Where first consonants more towards throat (h) and last letter more towards lips (p) to be more optimistic, If was the other way round were pessimistic. Treatment of age levels; For males first consonants h corresponding to care for young or last consonant p corresponding to recycling of elderly, For females first consonant p corresponding to discipline in relation to children and h corresponding to carelessness. [I will complete the remainder of the 7 parts of this naming code when I have more time and epiphanies;

2-REAL ESTATE;

Builder; consonants-

1st not throat, 2nd not back, 3rd only front, 4th only lips; vowels- First long, Last short.

Place; consonants-

1st only back, 2nd only front, 3rd not lips, 4th not throat; vowels- First short, Last long.

Hardware; consonants-

1st only throat, 2nd only back, 3rd , 4th not tongue; vowels- First mid, Last mid.

3-LIFE;

Herb; consonants-

1st only throat, 2nd not lips, 3rd , 4th only front; vowels- First short, Last short.

Microbe; consonants-

1st not front, 2nd only throat, 3rd , 4th only lips; vowels- First long, Last long.

Animal; consonants-

1st only lips,   2nd only front,   3rd   , 4 not throat;
vowels- First mid, Last mid.
4-FABRIC;
Clothes; consonants-
1st only front,   2nd not lips,   3rd not throat,   4th only back;
vowels- First short, Last short.
Linen; consonants-
1st,   2nd,   3rd,   4th;
vowels- First, Last.
Cleaning, towels; consonants-
1st only back,   2nd not throat,   3rd only front,   4th not lips;
vowels- First mid, Last short.
5-CARE;
Soap; consonants-
1st only lips,   2nd   , 3rd   , 4th not throat;
vowels- First short, Last mid.
Anti infection; consonants-
1st only throat,   2nd only lips,   3rd   , 4th last only front;
vowels- First short, Last long.
Nutrition; consonants-
1st not lips,   2nd only front,   3rd ,   4th only throat;
vowels- First long, Last mid.
6-INFOTECH;
Media; writings, video, radio, channels; consonants-
1st only lips,   2nd not front,   3rd,   4th only back;
vowels- First mid, Last mid.
Software programs; consonants-
1st only lips   2nd only throat, 3rd not front,   4th not back;
vowels- First long, Last short.
Currency; consonants-
1st only front,   2nd not lips,   3rd not back,   4th only throat;
vowels- First short, Last mid.
7-TOOLS; .
Vehicles; consonants-
1st only back,   2nd only lips,   3rd not throat,   4th only front;
vowels- First long, Last mid.
Tools to make things including computer, display, communications and meter; consonants-
1st only throat, 2nd not back,   3rd not front,   4th only lips;
vowels- First mid, Last short.
Weapons; consonants-
1st not back,   2nd only lips,   3rd not front,   4th only throat;
vowels- First mid, Last long.]

UNIVERSAL COLOR CODE:

BUILDINGS: White; walls, doors, ceilings, window frames. Black; built in kitchen bench top, toilet seat, seat as part of building, park bench with bolts into ground, seat component of taxi bus stop shelter. Red; heater, fire place. Blue; clean normal temperature water tank and pipes, water outlet. Yellow; lamp pole and socket for light bulb. Green; fence and sides of taxi-bus shelter. Orange; roof. Lilac purple cleaning and sanitation; sink, tub, toilet bowl and drains. Brown; doors both interior and exterior including of kitchen and bedroom cupboards as part of building, of postal box. Grey; exterior path, driveway, road. Clear; windows. Image; 2x mirrors slightly acute of right angle in corners. Natural; interior floors of timber and stone such as tiles.

CLOTHES: White; for shade; wide shade hat, shade shirt with long sleeves, shade pants. Black; socks including heater socks. Red; girl cool summer thin under layer, dress, shirt, underwear, skirt, shorts, pants and socks. Blue; man cool summer light weight short under layer short sleeve tee-shirt, polo shirt, under shorts and evaporative cooling vest. Yellow; writing such as rank insignia and "police" , "fire" , "emergency services" and "medic" also "convict" all over, police vest. Green; rain coat with rain hat and waterproof pants. Orange; rescue and safety, hi-viz work vest, radiation protection, safety vest, survival suit, life jacket, emergency services jacket, fire jacket, hard hat safety helmet. Lilac purple; girl thermally insulating coat, jacket, beanie, pants, gloves and socks for cold winter. Brown; Boots, shoes and sandals blend with natural. Grey; man thermally insulating coat, jacket, beanie, pants, gloves for cold winter. Clear; safety goggles. Image; photo identification pass. Natural; Boots, shoes and sandals natural cellular life components such as leather, wood and sheep skin blend with brown.

VEHICLES: White; passenger vehicle, people carrier, taxi, bus, train, aircraft, ferry, family car. Black; wheels, tires. Red; fire fighting, fire truck. Blue: police; cage car. Yellow; mining equipment, excavator, bulldozer, tunnelling machine. Green; farm machinery; tractor, harvester. Orange; rescue; ambulance, emergency services, tow truck, breakdown service. Lilac purple; garbage truck, sanitation vehicle, laundry van. Brown; cargo transport; container+bulk ship+train, parcel delivery van. Grey; military and free aid delivery; patrol boats, torpedo, fighter drone, missile, robot tank, personnel and aid carrier. Clear; window, wind shield. Image; display including from rear vision true image cameras and display. Natural; manual and weather power vehicles; canoe, sail boat, surfboard.

ELECTRONIC: White; wireless radio communications receiver and sender; antenna, radio sensor, radar, broadcast receiver box such as of television and radio, citizens bands ham radio frequency scanner receiver and transceiver (note; mobile worn electronics being all grey). Black; image display and photo scanner and audio speaker and microphone; video monitor display such as for television and computer, camera, photo printer, audio system speakers, desk phone, desk microphone. Red; alarm; fire alarm, burgled alarm, security system, warning light, siren. Blue; calculator, desktop and laptop computer, entertainment unit stream box. Yellow; measurement; electrical power meter, multi electronic meter, power meter, digital scales, electronic tape measure, electronic thermometer, table top and wall clock such as smart phone to use as a clock. Green; irrigation controller. Orange; door sensor alert, door bell, emergency rescue beacon such for boats, explorer and hikers, nurse call button in hospital, disabled medical assistance pendant call button. Lilac purple; toxic pollution hazard detector and alert; radiation detector, toxins such as drugs detection analyser, infections detection meter, road hazard sign with illumination, shop spillage slip hazard warning (light, text and sound). Brown; device memory data and information storage. Grey; mobile worn electronics; watch, headset, headphones, pocket mobile phone, mobile music player, hand hold and worn transceiver, pocket radio receiver. Clear: meter and innards window. Image; active screen. Natural; picture diagram.

CABLES; White; mains outer. Black; safe 23-25dc volts negative.

Red; safe 23-25dc volts positive. Blue; property and mains 220volts to 240volts alternating ac voltage neutral. Yellow; property and mains 220volts to 240volts alternating ac active hot. Green; ground from earth. Orange; high voltage dc outer with label. Lilac purple; high voltage dc positive. Brown; high voltage dc negative. Grey; 23-25dc volts and 2 fiber hybrid data and power cable outer. Clear; fiber optic core. Image; label tag. Natural; metal core.

SYMBOLIC SIGNALS, HANDLES AND BUTTONS; White; cooling button such as on water cooler cold tap handle, cooling button on air conditioner. Black; container lid on top such as of water bottle, food container and tool box. Red; heat button such as on (orange) hot water tap handle. Blue; normal temperature clean water such as on (orange) tap handle. Yellow; light switch. Green; power on button and go signal and sign. Orange; all handles, building handles, drawer handles, cupboard door handles, tool handles, blade handles. Lilac purple; drain, flush as on toilet and drain plug for basin, sink and tub. Brown; door lock keys. Grey; keys including keyboard unit, radio frequency tuning and volume dial knobs, for radio, computer, clock, phone, calculator, combination lock, also entire pointer device such as mouse including buttons and scroll wheel. Clear; chip circuit viewing window. Image; selfie photo on pass card. Natural; sun, moon and stars; seasons, time of day, tides and progress; cycles.

POWER EQUIPMENT; White; cooling; cooling air conditioner, fridge, fan. Black; power weapons such as firearm. Red; heater, microwave oven, furnace, stove, soldering iron, kiln, heat dryer, welder, hot water heater, kettle with own element, fire lighter, barbecue and electric + combustion stoves. Blue; Food appliances; blender, mixer, processor. Yellow; lighting; lamp base and light bulb. Green; gardening and agricultural power tools; lawn mower, chainsaw, chipper, cultivator. Orange; make and repair; industrial robot, press, cement mixer, nail staple gun. Lilac purple; cleaner; vacuum cleaner, washing machine, floor scrubber. Brown; power supply; battery, generator, energy collector, charge controller, inverter, power regulator, circuit breaker, rectifier, back of solar panels, compressor, pump, teleporter letter box. Grey; cutting, drilling, milling and sanding power tools. Clear; tool innards window. Image; screen on tool. Natural; wood for fire.

MANUAL TOOLS; White; stationary, stapler, paper hole punch, line ruler, writing paper, pen. Black; chair, table, desk, bed, table top of drawers. Red; fire extinguisher. Blue; cutlery, crockery, bowl, spoon, fork, food knife, drinking water bottle and food container, billy water bottle for fire and kettle for stove. Yellow; manual measure such as tape measure. Green; gardening, long handle pruning shears, pots, stakes, rake, hedge shears, fork, planting shovel, pick, weed grubber. Orange; making and repairing, hammer, screwdriver, paint brush. Lilac purple; cleaning and grooming, broom, scrubbing brush, scourer, mop, toothbrush, bucket, rubbish bin, laundry basket. Brown; tool box, parts bin, shipping container, cupboard including front of drawers. Grey; blades; knife, shaver, box cutter, scissors, chisel, grinder, saw, spear, paint removal scraper (note; green for garden and agricultural tools). Clear; mug, jug, water bottle in blend with blue. Image; photo and writing such as on paper. Natural; currency, bullion (matte).

LIFE: White; human skin blend with orange. Black; man body hair. Red; egg layer for food (chicken). Blue; eyes. Yellow; girl scalp hair. Green; plants. Orange; human skin blend with white. Lilac purple; flowers. Brown; soil. Grey; biological control agents; pollinators, cats, police and military guard and combat attack dogs, gray ET, bees. Clear; eye lens. Image; vision. Natural; food and water.

FABRIC: White; towel, tissue, toilet paper. Black; seating and under bedding; chair cover, fitting sheet for bed, pillow case. Red; carpet. Blue; outdoor fabric such as tent, awning, bladder water tanks and tubes. Yellow; interior curtains. Green; table cloth. Orange; bandage, band aid, wound cover. Lilac purple; female over bedding;

blanket, quilt, sleeping bag. Brown: bag, wallet, backpack, garbage bag. Grey; man over bedding, blankets, quilt, human shape sleeping bag. Clear; food wrap. Image; flag. Natural; wrapping paper.

144 Rights and protections of fair full Citizens born in a State of our Commonwealth nation: Shall extend to any location while residing in our Commonwealth nation more than have in any other single nation. If subsequently taking up citizenship or allegiance to another nation or illegal terrorist religion or gained our citizenship fraudulently, shall no longer have our Citizenship rights and protections.

145 Recognition of laws of States: Full faith and credit shall be given, throughout the Commonwealth to the laws the justice of every State subject to Royal Pardon.

146 Protection from invasion or violence: Every full citizen and resident shall have the responsibility and right to protect our Commonwealth nation and fair good citizens and residents from invasion or violence by blacks, fugitives, illegals, rapist, intoxicated, psychotic confused liars or any additional violent invader as the Governor General may define. Fair good full citizens without a criminal history shall for good reasons have the right to buy from a gun shop having accreditation of the local council to check and assess legal photo ID confirming citizenship and race, temperament, buyers online intelligence profile records online to add gun ownership particulars and with no other license or test have at any location unloaded standard arms (as the Federal Parliament shall determine) only to load to kill those assailants and vermin and put down disabled animals on own land and property plus at any location as the Governor General may authorise Attractive fair female citizens between the ages of 15 years and 35 years of age have the right at all places to own, carry and shoot dead black assailants such as rapists in self defence: standard .22 calibre bullet semi-automatic hand guns with laser pointer to aim. Black citizens as the Governor General shall select, pay and arm as rangers shall police and protect native title areas from invasion and deploy in any nation to fight foreign threats. The

Governor General may deploy up to 10,000 fair full citizens to each nation such as to man our embassies in English Commonwealth bases subject to approval of the countries legitimate democratic government. 147 Provision of cells and needs for detention of illegals, violent, intoxicated, psychotic or otherwise having term of incarceration by Police, Local Court, Military and Royal Tribunal: The Reserve Bank shall subject to Governor General issue new equal currency to all prison charity having accreditation from local council and over 95% occupancy to commission the construction and repair of a secure cell measuring more than 5 meters by 5 meters so that each prisoner have own cell with shower, toilet, basin with water drinking fountain, fresh air with temperature control, built in bed with under storage space and power point for electric blanket, built in table with leg room measuring more than 1m by 2m with power points for television ant lamp, secure door, food and provisions box to only open from each side when secure on the second door and secure ceiling. No hanging points. State shall make provision for the detention in its prisons of persons accused or convicted of offences against the laws of the Commonwealth, and for the punishment of persons convicted of such offences, and the Parliament of the Commonwealth may make laws to give effect to this provision. The Governor General may also commission construction of cells and open aid centres from the Fair English Language Commonwealth Empire military budget.

148 Government of native title area, External bases, embassies, protectorates and territories: The Parliaments may make laws native title areas so as to allow blacks to meat out own justice between each other along traditional tribal customs. Royal Tribunal of the Governor General shall set laws for governance of our external protectorates and territories as the English Commonwealth Monarchy Crown [Queen Elizabeth II] shall allocate.

148 Location of Parliaments, Local council chambers, Reserve Bank, and all national infrastructure. Shall be as the Governor General determines on advice from the Prime Minister, Premiers, ministers

and Mayors subject to funding and construction within 5 years.

149 Fair full citizens shall have the right to know and tell the truth.

150 Swearing in oath of affirmation:

I, [ ] do solemnly and sincerely affirm and declare that I will be faithful and bear true allegiance to the fair English Commonwealth Crown [Queen Elizabeth II] and heirs and successors according to populist law. SO HELP ME GOD!

All information between {} brackets is set by a 60% majority of a joint sitting of both houses of the national parliament unless otherwise indicated. All information between [] brackets is comment and has no legal affect on the constitution. All information between () brackets has the same consequence as the rest of the text.

END OF FAIR CHARTER: English Language Commonwealth Empire nations (CONSTITUTION)

----

www.ingramcontent.com/pod-product-compliance
Lightning Source LLC
Chambersburg PA
CBHW081302170526
45165CB00011B/3381